Attitude Is Everything

Also by Erik V. Sahakian

Shadowlands to the Songs of Seraphim

Check Yourself Before You Wreck Yourself

Where to Put the Ladder (co-author)

Don't Worry About a Thing

Attitude Is Everything

How to Choose a Biblical Perspective
in Times of Suffering

Erik V. Sahakian

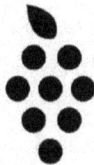

ABUNDANT HARVEST
PUBLISHING

Editing: McKenna Hafner
Cover Design/Layout: Andrew Enos

Library of Congress Control Number: 2021900269

ISBN 978-1-7349949-5-7
First Printing: March 2021

FOR INFORMATION CONTACT:

Abundant Harvest Publishing
35145 Oak Glen Rd
Yucaipa, CA 92399
www.abundantharvestpublishing.com

Printed in the United States of America

This book is dedicated to all those who are hurting, suffering, and struggling to hold on to their joy during these challenging times.

Contents

Oh, taste and see that the Lord is good; blessed is the man who trusts in Him!

Psalm 34:8

Preface

Collectively, the entire planet has gone through a fairly traumatic experience—the COVID-19 pandemic. And we're not out of the woods yet, since effects may linger for some time to come. Of course, in life, one challenge is always followed by another, so I believe the Lord placed this message of encouragement on my heart specifically for this season, but also for similar ones in years to come.

Everyone has experienced struggle, pain, and even suffering to varying degrees during this time. I don't think anyone has been exempt from being touched by some element of the pandemic—physically, financially, or emotionally. We've all taken a hit in some form or fashion.

That's reality, but it doesn't occur in a random vacuum. As followers of Jesus Christ, we know we are engaged in a supernatural conflict, not a physical one, though it impacts the physical universe. One element of this conflict is that we have a very real enemy whose intent is to rob us of our hope and joy.

Satan can't rob us of our salvation, but he'll try to rob us of everything else. He wants to insert hopelessness and depression into our mind. He wants to fill us with negative thoughts that the Lord has already given us power to overcome and transcend. Whether he succeeds or fails, however, is entirely our choice.

I wrote this book to convince you of the importance of choosing and maintaining an attitude of thankfulness, joy, and victory in the midst of struggle and suffering, and to share with you practical, biblical tools to equip you to do so.

So my prayer for us, as we embark on this journey together, is that we would take on the attitude of Job, who, when everything was taken away from him, was still able to say,

"The Lord gave, and the Lord has taken away; blessed be the name of the Lord" (Job 1:21).

In all honesty, praising the Lord when life seems to be inundated with difficulty and loss is a challenging mindset to maintain. Some may even believe it's impossible to have a worshipful perspective when your world is crashing down all around you. However, the Bible teaches that believers *do* have the supernatural ability to view our world, and the circumstances that affect us, with the same attitude of Job because we have the Holy Spirit in us!

Prior to sitting down to write this preface, I came across a scripture written by the hand of David that really ministered to me. In so many ways, it jumpstarted what I'm about to share with you throughout the remainder of this book. In Psalm 34:8, David writes,

"Oh, taste and see that the Lord is good; blessed is the man who trusts in Him!"

The phrase "taste and see" really jumped off the page at me. As I reflected upon this verse in my personal devotional time, I realized David was appealing to our human senses as a means of experiencing the goodness of God. Think about that for a moment—*taste* and *see* that the Lord is good. David is saying that God's goodness is on display *everywhere* for us to experience, if only we would engage with His goodness using the senses He gave us.

For example, even as I write this—in the spring of 2020, in the midst of a government ordered lockdown—I can look out my window and see that it is a gorgeous day. The birds, trees, and the sky aren't affected by the lockdown. Through this simple observation, I can measurably see the physical evidence of God's goodness in the world around me.

The second half of Psalm 34:8 says, "blessed is the man who trusts in Him!" The word "blessed" in Hebrew can actually be translated as "happy." In other words, happy is the man who trusts in God.

So we can experience true happiness when we trust in the Lord. Isn't that interesting? When we go through hard seasons we naturally become unhappy, but the path to happiness is trusting in God through the hard seasons. The very thing we need to do (trust) is the exact opposite of what we feel, but what we crave (happiness) won't come by doubting God, but by trusting Him. An eternal perspective helps us experience true happiness, and these days, we all could use a healthy dose of happiness!

Of course, our ability to trust in God is often linked to recognizing His goodness and faithfulness. When we recognize God's goodness, we are able to praise Him and give Him thanks. When we acknowledge God's faithfulness and trust in Him, we are then free to experience *true* happiness.

As we proceed, I've organized this book into three parts. In the first part, we'll address choosing a heart of thankfulness in the midst of adversity. In the second part we'll consider the work the Lord is doing in us through seasons of suffering, and why we must choose a mindset of joy in the process. Finally, in the last part, we'll focus on choosing a position of victory to overcome temptation in trials, because when we get caught up in the storm, instead of the Savior, we often find ourselves tempted to behave in ways we wouldn't normally consider.

Perhaps you sensed our theme—*choosing*. God doesn't change, we do. And changing is a choice. Therefore, the choice in the attitude we embrace is the difference between living a life of hope or hopelessness, joy or perpetual sorrow. It's the difference between living the abundant life that Jesus promised, or the pathetic façade the world offers instead. That's why I do believe that choosing the right attitude is everything.

Now let's begin…

Part One:

Choosing a Heart of Thankfulness

1

What is God's Desire?

Let's tackle our first question: *what* is God's desire when it comes to thankfulness? Does He even have a preference? Should we be drawn toward one mindset over another? Seriously, God's got a lot on His plate, so does our attitude even matter?

If you have been in church long enough, you probably already know the "churchy" answer is yes, God *wants* us to be thankful. Honestly, I think even people outside church would be able to guess that God prefers thankfulness over ingratitude. However, what many people may not realize is that it is actually God's *stated will* for us to be thankful.

First Thessalonians 5:16-18 says,

"Rejoice always, pray without ceasing, in everything give thanks; for this is the will of God in Christ Jesus for you."

That is pretty black and white, as crystal clear and no nonsense as you can get!

As Christians, we should spend prayerful time consciously seeking God's will for our lives. I think it's a worthwhile endeavor with a huge return on our investment to seek out the will of God and to walk in it. We should regularly be asking God what His will is for us. When we are faced with making an important decision, we should always seek the Lord's direction.

But sometimes we overcomplicate it, right? Or at least I do!

God Wills That We Will Seek His Will

Sometimes we treat God's will like it's a treasure at the end of a treasure hunt...something mysterious to be discovered. Now don't get me wrong, there are certainly life moments when we need to press in to hearing and understanding God's will for us. But He doesn't use His will as bait, or make it into a game like hide and seek.

Jesus tells us in Matthew 7:7-8,

"Ask, and it will be given to you; seek, and you will find; knock, and it will be opened to you. For everyone who asks receives, and he who seeks finds, and to him who knocks it will be opened"

Maybe you just read those verses and you're thinking, Wait, Pastor Erik, you just said God's will isn't a game of hide and seek, but those verses I just read specifically say, "he who seeks finds." So which is it?

God *does* give us a part to play, no doubt. He certainly wants our active involvement, but knowing His will is not a game. Look at what Jesus continues to say in the following verses,

"Or what man is there among you who, if his son asks for bread, will give him a stone? Or if he asks for a fish, will

he give him a serpent? In you then, being evil, know how to give good gifts to your children, how much more will your Father who is in heaven give good things to those who ask Him!" (Matthew 7:9-11).

When my children were very young, we used to play hide and seek, but I never really hid. I wanted to engage with them, I wanted interaction with my children, but they were young and it wouldn't have been fair for me to hide the way I'm truly capable of hiding. If I had done that then they never would have found me. So I pretty much hid in plain sight because I *wanted* them to find me!

God wants us to know His will for our lives and much of it is clearly revealed in Scripture. All we have to do is open our Bibles to find it. Many times, His will is revealed in general principles of wisdom for us to live by. Other times, it is expressly stated, like in First Thessalonians 5:16-18.

> *He will never withhold from you the knowledge of His will for you*

My encouragement to you is don't overcomplicate God's will. He will show you His will as you study the Bible and prayerfully seek Him. He will never withhold *from* you the knowledge of His will *for* you. God may not reveal everything you want to know in the timeframe you want to know it, but He will reveal what you need to know when you need to know it. Every day, day by day, His will for you will unfold like a blueprint of your life. All you have to do is seek Him.

So back to our question: what is God's desire when it comes to thankfulness?

First Thessalonians 5:16-18 clearly tells us that it is God's will that we be thankful,

"Rejoice always, pray without ceasing, in everything give thanks; for this is the will of God in Christ Jesus for you."

I think there are two key phrases here that are vital for our purposes moving forward. The first, as we've already established, is "this is the will of God." The second is "in everything."

We Can't Just Pick and Choose

God wants us to be thankful...not in a few things, but in *everything*. In other words, there is no exception to this rule. This may sound crazy at times, but there is never a reason for us not to give thanks to God.

Now, once again, in our humanity we may not *feel* like thanking God when life punches us in the gut, or kicks us when we're down. Though God deserves and desires our praise and thankfulness always, I still have moments where I feel defeated, discouraged, and depressed. God knows that I'm human and I don't believe that He faults me for those moments. Those are my very real *feelings*. But feelings do *not* determine reality, and what Scripture reveals is the reality that God is good all the time, and therefore always worthy of our praise and thankfulness.

When we get to chapter 4, we'll look at some practical ways we can give God thanks in everything, even when we're experiencing hard times. For now, I just want to establish that thankfulness is not something we should just pick and choose based on the moment, as if some moments require thankfulness and others do not. We do have a choice whether or not we choose to be thankful, but regardless of our choice, the Bible tells us that thankfulness is *always* warranted in all situations.

These two truths, that thankfulness is God's stated will and should be applied to everything, is the launch pad from which we will construct the rest of our perspective about thankfulness in troubled times.

2

Why Should We Give Thanks?

The second question we must ask is *why*. Why should we give thanks to God? Another way to think of this question is to ask, why is it God's will for us to give thanks in everything?

1. God is Good to Us All the Time

The first and foremost reason why it is God's will for us to give Him thanks is because He is good in His very nature, and He is good *to us* all the time! This is a given; God's goodness should never come into question. Even when trials, tribulation, and suffering arise, we must never permanently doubt the goodness of God.

In the preface, I mentioned Psalm 34:8, which says,

"Oh, taste and see that the Lord is good; blessed is the man who trusts in Him!"

This verse attests to the goodness of God. It doesn't say sometimes He is good, or maybe He is good; no, we are told He simply *is* good!

A second verse we can look to is Psalm 106:1, which reads,

"Praise the Lord! Oh, give thanks to the Lord, for He is

good! For His mercy endures forever."

We are to give praise and thanks to God because He is good and because His mercy endures forever. The bottom line is that God *never* ceases to be good.

Of course, bad things do happen, but not because of God. Bad things happen because we live in a broken and tainted world. All of humanity lives under a curse as a result of the fall in Genesis 3. It's not God's fault that this is the case. He did not cause Adam and Eve to sin, nor does man's sinfulness reflect poorly upon His goodness. God is good, and He is good all the time.

Admittedly, there are times in my life that I don't always feel that is the case. I can get caught up in my emotions and my circumstances the same as everybody else, but God's goodness transcends these things. His goodness even transcends our current circumstances.

Every single person on this planet has been affected in some way by the COVID-19 pandemic. My daughter finished her senior year of high school early so she could do overseas missions work. As a result of the pandemic, not only did she not get to experience a traditional graduation after years of hard work, but she can't travel overseas either. Other people have suffered far greater. Some have contracted the virus and fallen ill. Some have lost loved ones to the virus. Yet in the midst of all the pain and suffering of our current day, we must not let our emotions take away from our understanding of God's goodness.

Whose Side Are You On Anyway?

Recently, I was asked to teach the chapel service for the middle school at our church. The text I was given was Joshua 5:13-15. These verses take place right before Joshua is about to lead the children of Israel into the battle against Jericho.

While Joshua was taking a walk near Jericho, presumably overwhelmed by the enormity of the task before him, a christophany (pre-incarnate manifestation of Jesus) appeared before him. Here's what takes place in Joshua 5:13,

"And it came to pass, when Joshua was by Jericho, that he lifted his eyes and looked, and behold, a Man stood opposite him with His sword drawn in His hand. And Joshua went to Him and said to Him, 'Are You for us or for our adversaries?'"

That's a pretty relevant question, right? I mean, Joshua is probably feeling a bit anxious. He knows that God is on his side, but at the same time, this is the first battle he's leading since Israel crossed over the Jordan. Then suddenly this Man appears, with a sword drawn no less, and Joshua wants to know whose side is He on?

Check out the Man's response in verse 14,

"So He said, 'No, but as Commander of the army of the Lord I have now come.' And Joshua fell on his face to the earth and worshiped, and said to Him, 'What does my Lord say to His servant?'"

Isn't that amazing? Joshua asks, "Are You for us or for our

adversaries?" and the Man answers, "No."

Now, this didn't mean that God was impartial to the outcome of the pending battle. In fact, God had already determined that Jericho would fall. We read this just a few verses later, when God says in Joshua 6:2,

"See! I have given Jericho into your hand, its king, and the mighty men of valor."

Instead, I believe the reason the Man (Jesus) said "No" was because He was reminding Joshua that he wasn't calling the shots, God was calling the shots. Joshua wasn't in charge, the Commander of the army of the Lord was in charge! The real question wasn't whether God was on Joshua's side, it was whether Joshua was on God's side.

God had a much bigger, grander plan and the battle of Jericho was only a piece of it. Though God certainly cared about Joshua and the upcoming battle—He did show up with a sword drawn, after all—He was still Lord over the entire universe, not just the part that Joshua was in. Joshua needed to be reminded of that fact, which is why once he realized who he was talking to "Joshua fell on his face to the earth and worshiped, and said to Him, 'What does my Lord say to His servant?'"

Ah, now Joshua got their roles straight! Jesus was Lord, and Joshua was *His* servant.

You see, no matter what we face, through it all God will always be on the throne. He is greater, bigger, and still sovereign over all! Joshua may have been anxious, perhaps he was even a little afraid, yet God had already secured the victory for Israel. The battle was already won.

Our emotions are not truth and they will often betray us

This is why we can't surrender to our emotions. Our emotions are not truth and they will often betray us. We can't let our emotions determine our perception of God's goodness—God is good all the time!

A Practical Experiment

Here is a practical experiment to prove to you that God is truly good, gracious, and even generous, all the time. It's very simple and very applicable. All you have to do is take out a piece of paper and in one column write down all the blessings you see in your life. Go ahead. Grab a piece of paper and a pen, or write everything down on your computer or notes app.

Obviously, it goes without saying there may be things you wish were different in your life, and perhaps there are prayer requests you feel have gone unanswered, but set those realities aside for just a moment. Instead, choose to write down all your blessings. Consider the roof over your head, food in the refrigerator, money in the bank, and the health God has given you. Don't forget your family and friends who love you, the places you've traveled, the memories you've made, and the achievements you've accomplished.

Most importantly, write down that God has given you eternal life, the hope of heaven, a role in the family of God, and a calling on your life with gifts to match!

Now create a second column with those things you lack or are missing in your life. If we're being honest with ourselves, we'll quickly see that the side of the scale which weighs God's blessings far exceeds the side that measures what we lack.

Giving Credit Where Credit is Due

I've met some who give God no credit for many of these blessings. Rather, they attribute all the good things in their lives to themselves and their own diligence and ingenuity. I've had people try to tell me that God doesn't deserve the glory for their paychecks, for their promotions, and for any results they worked hard to achieve. They believe God wasn't the one who showed up to the office five days a week and clocked in, so why would He deserve any thanks?

Why *does* God deserve credit for all our blessing?

When such questions arise, I always take people to Acts 17:28. Tucked away in Paul's preaching to the Athenians in the Areopagus, we read,

"For in Him we live and move and have our being."

What does this mean? It means the very breath in our lungs comes from God. The animating force that gets us out of bed each morning is no credit to ourselves. The only reason we are even able to drive ourselves to work each day is because

God has given us the ability to. All credit and glory belong to Him!

If you don't believe me, then consider how every person is only one tragic accident away from easily losing whatever control or abilities they claim is their *own* doing. If those blessings truly originated from us, then they could never be taken away.

When I counsel people, I always try to encourage them to give God glory for everything in their lives. If you have health, praise the Lord. If you have a job that provides an income, praise the Lord. If you have food in your refrigerator, praise the Lord. If you have family, friends, and people who care about you, give glory to God. Sure, maybe you don't have as much money as you'd like, but if you have enough to make ends meet, thank Him. Maybe your house isn't your dream house, or the nicest one in the neighborhood, but if you have a roof over your head, praise God for His provision for you and your family.

God is good and He gives good blessings. We've touched on material blessings, but there are so many more! His blessings aren't always physical; they are mental, emotional, spiritual, and eternal, too!

In fact, we're told in James 1:17,

"Every good gift and every perfect gift is from above, and comes down from the Father of lights."

You might've heard this saying before, but it has always stuck with me since the day I first heard it. Earth is the *closest* a non-believer will ever get to heaven, but the *furthest* a believer will ever be from heaven. This is as bad as it's going to get for those who have the assurance of eternal life. We have nowhere to go but up. We have everything to look forward to!

Look at the Positive Side

God has given us eternal life. He has filled us with the Holy Spirit. He has empowered us with the gifts of the Holy Spirit. We get to be a part of a family, the body of Christ. Even when we cannot meet together, we are still knit together by the Holy Spirit.

Amidst the COVID-19 pandemic, I've seen this on full display. People are posting encouraging messages on social media, sending hope-filled texts to one another, and even conducting video meetings! The Holy Spirit has held our spiritual family together amidst all of the limitations on gathering.

You've probably experienced something similar if you've ever been on a mission trip to another country where there is a language barrier. You may not speak the same language, but there is a familiar love, a sense of family, and an inexplicable bond because of the indwelling of the Holy Spirit in each believer.

We have God with us 24/7. We are never alone. He never leaves us or abandons us. We have the hope of heaven and a blessed reunion with our loved ones to look forward to! All of these blessings attest to God's goodness and faithfulness.

They are proof of His great love for us. We give God our thankfulness because He is good *all the time.*

2. Thankfulness is an Act of Worship

The second reason we should give thanks is because thankfulness is an act of worship. We are called to worship God. In fact, it is our position as God's creation to worship Him. You could say it's in our job description to glorify Him as our Lord and Savior.

We see a great example of this in Psalm 54:6, which says,

"I will freely sacrifice to You; I will praise Your name, O Lord, for it is good."

All throughout Scripture there is a common theme of God's goodness. And because He is good in His very nature, and because He is God, He is always deserving of worship. So we are always called to worship God, but sometimes it costs us something. When we don't feel like worshiping, yet we worship out of obedience anyway, we worship Him with thankful hearts as an act of *sacrifice.*

Just as there are moments when our emotions may get the better of us, and we may feel like God isn't good, there are also moments when we don't feel like worshiping or thanking Him. It could be due to unresolved sin in our lives, believing the enemy's lies, or because we haven't been properly spending time at the feet of Jesus. If we're being honest, sometimes we don't worship just because we're distracted, tired, or lazy! For whatever reason, sometimes we come to church and thanksgiving and praise are just not stirring in our hearts.

Perhaps that has been the case in this season as we've watched church online from our homes. I think every Christian would agree that corporate worship is not the same experience on your television or laptop, as it is when we are physically together in a group. Due to the differences, maybe you've found yourself resisting the call to allow yourself to enter into a mindset of worship. Maybe you haven't been singing along in worship because it feels silly or awkward.

This is why we must realize that ultimately the battle to overcome our emotions begins in the mind.

Garbage In, Garbage Out

I remember my freshman year of high school I picked up a secular book that was very dark in content. Not long after beginning the book, I began to sense that the days seemed to be gloomy and dark, too. I wasn't feeling like myself either. I was moody, out of sorts, and depressed. This went on steadily for two whole weeks. I kept trying to figure out what was different in my life, when it finally struck me that the nature of the book was affecting my perception of the world around me. I didn't bother finishing the book; instead, I threw it in the trash. I literally felt better after that!

There is an old computer programming term that states, "garbage in, garbage out." The phrase refers to the correlation between bad input data resulting in bad output data. In other words, if you program junk into the computer, the computer will just kick out junk as well. When you think about it, the same is true of the human mind.

As followers of Jesus Christ, who have been bought with the price of His precious blood, we need to ask ourselves, what kinds of things are influencing our perspective? Are our minds fully submitted to Christ?

In Philippians 4:8, Paul writes,

"Finally, brethren, whatever things are true, whatever things are noble, whatever things are just, whatever things are pure, whatever things are lovely, whatever things are of good report, if there is any virtue and if there is anything praiseworthy—meditate on these things."

In contrast, if you turn the above list to its opposite (whatever things are untrue, impure…etc.), we see exactly what we are *not* to allow our minds to meditate or dwell on. Paul's exhortation should be the test by which we weigh the various interests that compete for the attention of our minds.

In Romans 12:2, Paul writes,

"And do not be conformed to this world, but be transformed by the renewing of your mind."

Have you ever wondered how we are to renew our minds? Let's begin with what we put into our minds. After all, the things which are planted into our minds are what manifest themselves in our actions. Galatians 6:8 states,

"For he who sows to his flesh will of the flesh reap corruption, but he who sows to the Spirit will of the Spirit

reap everlasting life."

Jesus wants His bride, the Church, to be holy and without blemish. So let's be conscious about the conflicting thoughts we may have regarding worship and thankfulness. Those feelings may be real, but that doesn't make them true. Remember, garbage in, garbage out.

Pressing In and Pushing Through

In this season and in those to come, we must transcend. We must press in and push through. That's how sacrifice works. It isn't meant to be easy, but we honor, thank, and praise God in doing so. Our thankfulness must not be based on our feelings. It must be based on who God is and what He has done. We must push past our feelings and ascend to a place of gratitude.

> *Christians should be the most*
> *thankful and worshipful people*
> *on earth because we have*
> *every reason to be both*

Once again, refer back to your list of blessings and allow your heart to flood with thankfulness as you see all God has given you, even in difficult seasons. Resist focusing on the negative and what is lacking. That is a very unhealthy place for us to be as Christians. Instead, shift your thinking and move into a posture of thankfulness. Strive for a worshipful mindset. Allow the Holy Spirit to stir up godly desires within you so that you can honor and glorify the Lord.

Christians should be the most thankful and worshipful people on earth because we have every reason to be both. Unlike those who are going through this worldwide pandemic without the assurance of eternal life, we have the hope, joy, and power of the Holy Spirit through Jesus Christ. We have God's Word. We have the body of Christ for encouragement. We have absolutely everything we need to express our worshipful thanks to God amidst a difficult season.

3. An Ungrateful Heart is a Sinful Heart

The third reason we should be thankful is because an ungrateful heart is a sinful heart. Let that sink in for a moment. If needed, let it even convict you. An ungrateful heart is actually a *sinful* heart. The apostle Paul writes in his letter to the Roman church,

"Although they knew God, they did not glorify Him as God, nor were thankful, but became futile in their thoughts, and their foolish hearts were darkened" (Romans 1:21).

Isn't that interesting? Paul is saying that those who were not thankful and did not give God glory were led into a mindset of futile thinking. In turn, they were led into total foolishness.

Have you heard the saying, "sin makes you stupid"? According to Romans 1, being unthankful is a sin and it leads us to foolish thinking, which then leads to foolish behavior. That is exactly where the enemy wants us to be. He wants us to take our eyes off the ball.

Keep Your Eyes on the Ball

If you have ever played baseball or softball, you know that if you take your eyes off the ball, one of two things may happen. You are either going to miss the ball completely or you are going to get hit *by* the ball. The enemy doesn't want us to knock the ball out of the park. He wants to distract us with futile, foolish thinking, as Paul says.

To be unthankful is to deny God's goodness and glory— that's the reason it's sin

To be unthankful is to deny God's goodness and glory— that's the reason it's sin. That's why we must resist not being thankful. Of course, it is our natural human tendency to be unthankful. Every single person is guilty.

Even as I write these words, I raise my hand in acknowledgement with you. Though we are all guilty, we don't have to be chained by our failures. Don't stay in a mindset of being unthankful. Return your focus to the goodness of God. Don't deny His goodness by refusing to give Him thanks. Don't deny Him the glory He is due by withholding your gratitude.

The World is Watching

An unthankful mindset also misrepresents the character and nature of God. If we have an unthankful attitude or thoughts, it will eventually translate into unthankful actions. The internal will always manifest itself externally. An unthankful mindset will eventually rear its ugly head in a very public way. In doing so, we misrepresent God, His goodness, and His glory.

Second Corinthians 5:20 calls us to be ambassadors for Christ and the gospel. Consider that we are supposed to represent Him with our lives:

"Now then, we are ambassadors for Christ, as though God were pleading through us: we implore you on Christ's behalf, be reconciled to God."

You may not think anyone is paying attention. You may think you are in the clear, but I can guarantee you that someone will take notice. Especially in times as difficult as these, the world is paying attention to how Christians are reacting. They want to see how we respond when it gets hot in the kitchen. They are waiting to see if we are going to act out in the flesh, or if we are going to act out in faith.

Believer, don't forget that we are under a greater microscope than ever before. If we are unthankful or ungrateful, we will misrepresent who God is to the world around us. In our renewed hearts, I know that we would never intentionally want to do that, but sometimes we forget when the enemy clouds our minds.

Satan doesn't want us to recognize the traumatic and regretful consequences of an ungrateful posture. Don't let him damage the witness you have to the world around you. People who are lost, without hope or joy, apart from Christ, are desperately watching.

Give thanks because God is good all the time.

Give thanks because thankfulness is an act of worship.

Give thanks because an ungrateful heart is a sinful heart.

3

When Do We Give Thanks?

The third question we must answer is *when* do we give thanks. Fortunately, Scripture is abundantly clear on this too. Ephesians 5:20 tells us,

"Giving thanks always for all things to God the Father in the name of our Lord Jesus Christ."

In short, we are supposed to give thanks *all the time.*

This speaks to a constant mindset of appreciation and gratitude. As I've admitted before, I struggle with this. Everyone does. That's our reality as sinful human beings. What we must remember is that God is always working. He never takes a break. He's on the job 24 hours a day, 7 days a week. Whether we recognize it, feel it, or see it, He is always moving.

How Fast Does the Earth Spin?

Some time ago, I was thinking on this very fact—that God is often doing things behind the scenes that we don't even realize. It made me curious about the earth spinning on its axis. We usually don't give this much thought, although we're vaguely aware of its effects with the changing hours of the day. So out of curiosity I did some research. Do you know how fast the earth spins? It's spinning at roughly 1,000 miles per hour! Yet we don't feel it, we don't hear it, and we don't see it.

Have you ever truly considered that God is similar, but on a much grander and majestic scale? That He is moving and working in a massive way, yet for the most part it defies our awareness and senses?

> *God is taking care of us all the time, not just on the rare occasions when we realize it*

Our gratitude is often a reaction to something that has happened to us. We tether it to our consciousness and senses, but that's exactly what leads us to miss all that God is doing. The reality is that God is taking care of us all the time, not just on the rare occasions when we realize it.

For example, when you are sick, you probably ask God to heal you, and when He does you praise Him. But what if you are sick and you don't even know it, and He heals you? You wouldn't automatically think to thank Him because you didn't even know you had been healed. Or spared a tragic car accident, or been protected from an unhealthy relationship. You get the idea.

I came across an example of this in the Bible that was right under my nose, yet had gone unnoticed so many times. In premarital training of engaged couples, I always start them off with Genesis 2:18, which states,

"And the Lord God said, 'It is not good that man should be alone; I will make him a helper comparable to him.'"

Pretty straight forward and to the point, right?

Then one day it hit me. There's no biblical evidence that Adam was knowingly unhappy or dissatisfied with his situation. He was living in a perfect environment, had a life of meaning and purpose, and he had direct fellowship with God. What was there to complain about?

Yet, Genesis 2:18 clearly tells us that God recognized there was something profoundly missing from Adam's life, so He stepped in (unbeknownst to Adam) and resolved the situation. One moment Adam was without a partner, he takes a nap, and *BOOM*, wakes up no longer alone! God moved on Adam's behalf to bless and provide for him, all before Adam even knew it was happening.

You see, God is doing far more than we often realize. He's like the earth, spinning at 1,000 miles per hour ALL the time, and we're just walking about our daily lives, largely oblivious about it!

For this reason, Ephesians 5:20 reminds us that we are called to be "giving thanks always for all things to God." He is always moving in our lives to accomplish His good purposes, which is why we should be giving thanks at all times.

Of course, sometimes our life circumstances and emotions

get in the way of this.

Four Bald Tires and a Dream

There is a great illustration I'm going to share with you that involves another pastor at my church. Truth be told, Pastor Matt is probably tired of me sharing this story all the time, but I can't help myself. He has probably lost his blessing in heaven for it due to the amount of times I've shared it with others! However, it perfectly fits the picture of the natural man's mindset in relationship to God's constant faithfulness.

Years ago, before Matt and I were ever pastors at Wildwood Calvary Chapel, we were simply friends.

One day, my wife, Juanita, and I were driving our son, Maksim, to school. At the time, we were struggling financially since I had left my business to pursue vocational ministry (you can read more about that experience in my book, *Don't Worry About A Thing*). We were quite literally living paycheck to paycheck. Looking back, in all honesty, that probably wasn't even enough; we were short every single paycheck. We were struggling so much that we had to drive Maksim to school in a borrowed vehicle because we couldn't afford one of our own.

In the middle of our drive, one of the tires blew out. Fortunately, we were just around the corner from the school and were still able to drop him off, but I remember getting out of the car and seeing that the damaged tire was irreparable. It was especially depressing since the other tires were also in bad condition and ready to blow at any moment. Even if we could scrounge up the money to fix the one tire, we'd soon have to find a way to replace the other three as well.

Matt worked at Maksim's school at the time. When he saw me, he ran over to help me put the spare on. I remember going home afterward with Juanita, both of our spirits completely crushed.

We walked in the door, went straight to the couch, and sat on opposite sides, as far away from each other as possible! We weren't angry with each other—neither of us did anything wrong—but we were both down in the dumps and taking it out on the other. We didn't talk. We didn't even turn the TV on. We simply sat on opposite sides of the couch in silence and moped.

I can't tell you exactly what was going through her mind, but the thoughts in my head were pretty bummed. I was depressed. I felt as though I wasn't a good husband or father. I was beating myself up and thinking negatively about it all.

The ironic part of this story is that, at some point, I happened to pick up my phone and saw a text message waiting to be opened. Matt's wife, Angela, had sent me a text nearly an hour earlier, but I'd been too busy feeling sorry for myself to notice. The message informed me that Juanita and I were to go to a specific tire shop in town the next day and get four brand-new tires *for free*. Angela wrote that she and Matt had worked it out with a bunch of people from church to bless us with what we needed.

In that moment, I realized two convicting truths: an ungrateful heart is a sinful heart and a lack of thankfulness leads to foolish behavior.

Problem Solved

I felt like such a fool for wasting an hour of my life feeling sorry for myself unnecessarily. In reality, the problem had already been solved. This is the reality in *every* situation. Maybe you don't have the exact solution written out in a text on your phone, but God already knows how everything is going to work out.

> In God's sovereignty, He has already solved every problem you will ever face before the problem has even arrived

If you've lost your job, God already knows how He will provide for you next. If you are struggling in your marriage, God knows how He is going to bring healing. God has already made an avenue for us to walk down if only we choose to seek, follow, and pursue Him.

The answers are already there for us to grasp. The solution is ready for us to find hidden in His Word. Consider that in God's sovereignty, He has already solved every problem you will ever face before the problem has even arrived.

This might seem overly simplified, but I think of God's

perspective, versus man's perspective, using the illustration of a parade symbolizing one's life. If you've ever been to a parade, you know that you can only see a limited distance in either direction. You can't see the float that is turning the corner a quarter mile away, or sometimes what is even down the street. You can only see and experience a limited amount of space at a time. Yet, God sees from the vantage point of a hovering helicopter. He sees the entire parade, your life, in one view, while you can only see it one moment at a time.

Man is stuck in time and space, but God transcends both. He already knows how your entire life story will play out, but you only see page by page, chapter by chapter. Because of this, we should give thanks to God all the time in everything.

We may not be able to see how God is working it out, but we must trust that He is working it out on our behalf. We must show our thankfulness in faith that God is going to bring us the solution, the direction, and the victory. We can be thankful not only for what He has *already* done, but for what He is *going* to do in the future.

"But without faith it is impossible to please Him, for he who comes to God must believe that He is, and that He is a rewarder of those who diligently seek Him."

– Hebrews 11:6

4

How Do We Give Thanks?

The final question we need to answer is *how* do we give thanks. What are some practical ways that we can express our thankfulness to God as a testimony to the world? There are three ways I want to look at specifically that I think will prove to be a great help in this difficult season and those to come.

1. Giving Thanks Through Our Words

The first practical way that we can give thanks is through our words. Paul says in Philippians 4:6,

"Be anxious for nothing, but in everything by prayer and supplication, with thanksgiving, let your requests be made known to God."

Paul is telling us that even while we're praying and bringing our supplications to God, we should *still* give Him thanks.

You may be asking what that looks like practically. Let's say, for instance, you're struggling to pay your mortgage. How do you give thanks to God at the same time that you're asking Him for provision? Here's what I would suggest: while you're praying to God and asking Him for help or guidance, at the same time, you can also be thanking Him for what He has *already* blessed you with and how He will answer your prayers in the future.

Here is an example…

Dear Jesus, You know I can't afford the mortgage this month because my job came to an end. However, thank You for the fact that I have a mortgage at all. It is proof that my family has a roof over our heads. Thank You for this home that You've blessed us with. Thank You for this home that You've allowed us to stay in. Thank You for providing the means to make the mortgage payment all these years.

Even though I'm struggling this month, I believe by faith that You're always faithful, even though I never deserve it. So I believe that You're going to continue to lead my family in Your will, wherever our home is located. If You want us to stay here, please provide the resources to make the payment, but if not, please give me wisdom to see where You're guiding us next. Amen.

In every single one of our prayer requests, there should always be something we are thanking God for

Do you see how even in the midst of acknowledging a need or an area of struggle, we can still thank God for what He has done and for what He will do? We can speak out in faith, believing that He will be faithful to answer our prayers according to His will. In every single one of our prayers requests, there should always be something we are thanking God for. Pray to God, bring your requests to Him, but don't leave out words of gratitude and praise. Acknowledge His goodness by thanking Him for what He has done in your life.

God has never stopped being good, nor will He ever stop being good. He always deserves our praise, glory, and worship. Thankfulness is always a proper response to His goodness. We show God that we are thankful through our words in prayer.

2. Giving Thanks Through Our Actions

The second way we can give thanks to God is through our actions. In Colossians 3:17, Paul says,

"And whatever you do in word or deed, do all in the name of the Lord Jesus, giving thanks to God the Father through Him."

In my Bible, I underlined the words *whatever* and *do all*. The statement "whatever you do" is very broad, but it summarizes every capacity we have. All of those things we have the ability to do, we must do with thankfulness. People may or may not hear our words, but they will see our actions.

I don't know if you do the same, but I always talk out loud to myself. Especially when I'm alone, I'm talking. However, people may not hear my words, but they can see my actions. As the saying goes, actions speak louder than words. What are your actions showing people? What message are you sending? Is it one of faith? Is it one of thankfulness?

Faith or a Lack of Faith?

There's a great example of the message our actions send to others regarding our faith. We find it in Matthew 8:23-26, which reads,

"Now when He got into a boat, His disciples followed Him. And suddenly a great tempest arose on the sea, so that the boat was covered with the waves. But He was asleep. Then His disciples came to Him and awoke Him, saying, 'Lord, save us! We are perishing!' But He said to them, 'Why are you fearful, O you of little faith?' Then He arose and rebuked the winds and the sea, and there was a great calm."

In the midst of a crazy storm—a storm where the waves were actually covering the boat—Jesus was so unimpressed that He was actually asleep! However, His disciples believed they were about to die. In fact, the Greek word for "perishing" is *apollumi*, which can also be translated "to destroy fully."

It is important to keep in mind that some of those men were professional fishermen. They were not novices. They had the knowledge and experience to know the difference between a serious storm and a mild one. They would know if their lives were truly in danger or not. And in this particular storm, their collective experience told them they were about to be annihilated.

[50]

Yet when they aroused Jesus from His sleep, His response was to rebuke them for their faithlessness. Then he rebuked the wind and sea, and everything was calm. Easy-peasy.

> *When we let an unthankful attitude take root in our lives, it will spill out into our actions and we will misrepresent God to those around us*

When we are unthankful, it will show in our actions. The message will be sent to our spouse, our kids, our relatives, our friends, our coworkers, our neighbors…to everyone! When we let an unthankful attitude take root in our lives, it will spill out into our actions and we will misrepresent God to those around us.

When we show a lack of faith through our actions, we are discrediting God's goodness and casting doubt on His glory. I would even go so far as to say that we're diminishing God's power. Now obviously we don't *literally* have the capacity to take away from God's power, but that's the image we are projecting with our actions.

The message we're sending is that we doubt God's ability. That's the message the actions of the disciples were delivering to Jesus, even as their words were asking Him to save them. See? They asked for the right thing in words of faith ("Lord, save us!"), but their actions betrayed their actual lack of faith ("We are perishing!"), and Jesus called them on it ("O you of little faith"). Our actions do speak louder than our words.

For those who don't know any better, for the nonbeliever looking into your life, that misrepresentation could be very detrimental to their understanding of God. Be mindful of your words. Be mindful of your actions. There will always be people watching, whether it's at home, in the workplace, in the classroom, in the neighborhood, at the gym, and on the sports field. The world is always watching those who claim to follow Jesus Christ. They want to see if we are the real deal. The want to know if our actions back up our words.

I'm speaking to you from a position of experience. I've messed up. I'm guilty of misrepresenting God. We all are. If you think you aren't, you're mistaken. That's why it would benefit us to be mindful of our message. Scripture actually calls us to self-reflect and ask ourselves certain questions (First Corinthians 11:28; Second Corinthians 13:5).

What is the world seeing us doing in the midst of difficult trials? Are we running around in a panic, like chickens with our heads cut off, like the disciples in Matthew 8? Or are we relying on and trusting in God who is faithful and good?

3. Giving Thanks Through Our Attitude

The third way we can give thanks to God is through our attitude. People don't necessarily see our attitude, but they certainly see the *manifestation* of our attitude. I saved the best for last because the three points in this chapter are intentionally presented in reverse order. You could say that everything begins with attitude, which then manifests itself in our actions, and then spills out through our words. So we're purposefully ending with the beginning to make the point more poignant.

Psalm 9:1-2 tells us,

"I will praise You, O Lord, with my whole heart; I will tell of all Your marvelous works. I will be glad and rejoice in You; I will sing praise to Your name, O Most High."

The phrase *I will praise you, O Lord* is also underlined in my Bible. I want that to be my motto, no matter what is going on in my life. In all honesty, sometimes I have to convince myself, which is okay. If you have to drill this into your brain until it sinks in, do it. If you have to keep reminding yourself, do it. Our sinful nature will keep resisting, so we have to keep resisting right back! We're like cars on bumpy roads that need to be realigned over and over again.

When Scripture speaks about the heart, it is sometimes speaking about the heart that is beating within us. However, most of the time it is referring to the heart as the seat of our emotions, will, and intellect—our very being. So when you read Psalm 9:1-2, David is really saying, "I will praise You, O Lord, with my *whole being*…with everything that I am, with the immaterial part of my self, with my thoughts, feelings, and emotions." That's what this verse is getting at. It is a beautiful picture of a thankful heart, a grateful heart, and a worshipful heart.

Our actions tell people what we do, but our attitude tells people who we are and, as a result, who God is to us. We are ambassadors and representatives of Him. If I have a distrustful attitude toward God, I am telling the world that God is unworthy of my trust. Guard your heart. Guard your mind. Guard your being. Don't allow negative, unthankful thinking to manifest itself in the wrong words and actions. Stop yourself before you misrepresent God to nonbelievers who desperately need Him. Don't let it take away from the effectiveness of your witness.

A Change of Perspective

On our church property there is a cross that is secured into the ground. It serves as a place for people to seek God, to pray, and to meet in fellowship. Years ago, in a season of life inundated with uncertainties and questions, I went to the cross.

At the time, I didn't know whether we were going to lose our home (that wasn't just a hypothetical sample prayer I shared earlier!), since the Lord had called me to give away my business and follow Him into vocational ministry. I didn't know whether Juanita would remain supportive of this decision once the full ramifications set in. I wasn't sure if our children, Skylar and Maksim, understood why our standard of living drastically changed. I didn't want them to be resentful toward me, toward the church, and especially toward God. I didn't want them to blame God for the sacrifices we'd have to make as a family in the days, months, and years to come.

So I stood at the cross, pouring my heart out to God with one "what if" after another. In that moment, God spoke very clearly to me in my spirit—*Erik, you can focus on what you don't know, or you can focus on what you do know. What do you know?*

I took out my phone and opened up my notes application. I started typing out all the things I knew to be true. It soon became a list of amazing blessings that attested to the goodness of God. Of course, by the time the list was finished, there were still *many* things I didn't know. I didn't know if we'd be able to make our mortgage payments. I didn't know if we'd eventually lose our house. I didn't know if we'd eventually lose our vehicles. I literally had no idea what the future had in store for my family.

You can focus on what you don't know, or you can focus on what you do know

---

However, God's will for my thoughts was very clear to me. He didn't want me focusing on life's uncertainties; He wanted me to focus on His faithfulness and promises—blessings I could be certain about in a time of much uncertainty. My list was filled with amazing examples and though the app and the phone it was on are long gone, the list is etched in my memory...

- I know I am a child of God
- I know I am going to heaven
- I know I am called to live in Yucaipa, California
- I know I am called to be a husband
- I know I am called to be a father
- I know I am called to serve the community
- I know I am called to be a pastor

At the time of writing this list, I wasn't yet ordained as a pastor, but God's calling on my life was unmistakably clear. He had called me to leave my business and be available to serve, believing that one day He would make me a pastor. God eventually fulfilled that calling in my life and, all these years later, I can't imagine doing anything else. I love being a pastor at Wildwood. I love this flock. I wake up every day and pinch myself because I can't believe this is my job.

As I look back on that day in 2012, I still vividly remember writing down the list. Amazingly, as soon as I did, my attitude changed. My perspective flipped. I immediately became thankful the moment I recognized the goodness of God in my life!

You see, focusing on uncertainty only breeds more uncertainty, but focusing on God's faithfulness will build up your faith every single time. The choice is ours, but God's will is abundantly clear. He proclaims in Isaiah 46:9,

"Remember the former things of old, for I am God, and there is no other; I am God, and there is none like Me."

His goodness is never absent, but sometimes we are blind

to it. We can become oblivious when we begin to focus on peripheral circumstances, and fear begins to overtake our hearts. Sometimes we may even deny His goodness because we're focusing on the storm, and not the anchor in the storm.

However, the solution isn't complicated—we just need a change of perspective, a realignment of truth into our lives, and what will follow is an attitude of thankfulness and praise. I believe that if you take the time to do what God told me to do that day at the cross, to write down all the things that are evidence of His goodness in your life, to "remember the former things of old" that He has already accomplished in your life, your soul will be overwhelmed with gratitude and worship every single time.

5

Changing Our Heart

Years ago, I had the privilege of teaching, at a local elementary school, a technology class for third graders in the afternoon. I remember giving them an assignment for Thanksgiving, asking them to write on their laptops all the things they were thankful for.

Now, most of them wanted to write down their Christmas "wish lists" instead, but after some lawyerly negotiating we stuck with the plan! It was a blast reading their responses, but it was even more fun to watch them brighten as they recognized all the ways they were already blessed (take *that* Christmas wish lists!).

It's no secret that the reality is no one's life is perfect. At any given moment, we can all list off several areas of our lives that we wish were different or better, but what about all the blessings we already have? Life is a mixed bag of days where we are on top of the world and other days where we are face-down in the mud!

Hopefully by this point you're convinced that the key to choosing a heart of thankfulness is to maintain a biblical perspective of life, both the good and the bad. Here are two simple tools, taken right out of God's Word, that if we were to master in our thinking, would totally change our hearts and turn them toward deep and profound thankfulness toward God.

1. Learn to Be Content

I like what Paul says in Philippians 4:11-12, when he states,

"Not that I speak in regard to need, for I have learned in whatever state I am, to be content: I know how to be abased, and I know how to abound. Everywhere and in all things I have learned both to be full and to be hungry, both to abound and to suffer need."

Notice, twice Paul uses the word "learned" to describe the process of arriving at contentment. Contentment doesn't just happen; we have to *learn* how to be content. You see, Paul's not living in denial about the down times; instead, he is acknowledging both the good and the bad. It's the full experience of life, the ups and the downs, that should cause us to appreciate what we've been given.

It reminds me of a statement that President Nixon said in his final speech as he was stepping down in disgrace from his presidency: "Only if you have been in the deepest valley, can you ever know how magnificent it is to be on the highest mountain." How true.

When we have an eternal perspective, versus a temporal one, our entire mindset and attitude about our circumstances is different. That's why Paul's next statement is so important:

"I can do all things through Christ who strengthens me"
(Philippians 4:13).

That verse is very encouraging in its broad application to all kinds of challenges in life (overcoming sin, kicking a bad habit, accomplishing a major goal), but in its specific context what Paul is actually referring to is that God is the source of our strength to be content in any situation. If I may paraphrase what Paul is saying in Philippians 4:11-13, it's that Jesus gives us the strength to be content in every situation. Contentment is the key to thankfulness, and Jesus is the key to contentment.

2. Acknowledge All Blessings

When we keep our eyes on Jesus we're reminded that every blessing we have is an undeserved gift of grace, so when trials or setbacks come, we can recognize that those hardships are swallowed up by the sheer volume of everything good that He has given us. This is why Job was able to say, even in the apparent midst of losing everything,

"The Lord gave, and the Lord has taken away; blessed be the name of the Lord" (Job 1:21).

That's an eternal perspective!

It's nearly impossible to deny that, even in the hard times, there is always much to be thankful for. The scale is always off balance in favor of our blessings. You may have an unfair boss, but at least you're employed. Your house may be a total mess, but at least you have a home. Your body may be out of shape, but at least you're alive!

We have a sign hanging in our laundry room that says, "I am thankful for piles of laundry…it means my loved ones are nearby." The truth is each of us is supremely blessed, but

> *It's not what happens to us in life that defines us—it's how we respond*

we have to make a decision to acknowledge that truth.

So do we praise God only when we are pleased with life's outcomes, but curse Him when our plans fall apart? Or do we give God thanks even in the bad times, knowing that He is using those tough times to make us better? It's not what happens to us in life that defines us—it's how we respond.

The emotion of thankfulness comes and goes with the tide, but the mindset of being thankful doesn't. If we can 1) learn to be content by the strength of Christ, and 2) consistently choose to acknowledge our blessings, then we'll have unlocked the secret to choosing a heart of thankfulness, no matter what life throws our way!

Part Two:

Choosing a Mindset of Joy

6

Where Does Joy Begin?

Some years back, I had to go on a business trip to New York for three weeks. Although it was an incredible experience, it was a struggle for me to be away from my family for such a long period of time. I can vividly recollect the anticipation of the plane ride home. I remember coming down the escalator at Ontario International Airport with my luggage under one arm and a doll for my daughter, Skylar (who was a toddler at the time), under the other. At the bottom of the escalator, near the baggage claim, I could see my family waiting for me with balloons and smiles.

I will never forget the joy of greeting Skylar as she fell completely into my arms. There are no words to express how good it felt to be home. Sometime later, I saw a photo of the moment Skylar and I greeted each other, seconds before we embraced. The look of pure, unadulterated joy captured on her little face brought me to tears. I've never seen anything quite like it, before or since.

The Unlikeliest Place for Joy—the Cross

As beautiful and perfect as that moment of joy shared with my daughter was, it pales in comparison to the joy that comes as a result of Jesus Christ's finished work on the cross. It's one of history's greatest poetic ironies that a blood-stained cross, an object of brutal, torturous suffering and pain, could be the starting line for a lifetime of joy in our lives. Scripture testifies to this truth in Hebrews 12:2, in speaking of Jesus,

"Who for the joy that was set before Him endured the cross, despising the shame, and has sat down at the right hand of the throne of God."

Whose joy was set before Jesus? Our joy. It was for our joy that He endured the shame of the cross. He didn't die on the cross for His benefit, He died on the cross for ours.

> *Christians should be the most joyful people on the planet because we have a lasting joy that is a result of our salvation in Christ*

That's why apart from the cross, there would be no lasting joy for us because we would still be slaves to sin, with a chasm separating us and God. Yet because of the cross, we are now free from the bondage and shackles of sin. We are no longer separated from God and we will one day go home to be with Him forever! No other joy can compare to being reunited with our Creator who fashioned and formed us, to be in fellowship with Him—no more separation, no more distance, no more chasm—for eternity!

There are so many reasons for us to be joyful, and they all begin with the cross...

- A restored relationship with God, the source of joy
- Forgiveness of our sins
- A new identity as a child of God
- A new purpose in life as a servant of God
- The hope of eternal life in heaven

The list can literally go on and on, but every reason we have to be joyful is ultimately found in Jesus and His cross.

Experiencing the Fullness of Joy

So joy starts at the cross, but how do we experience it on a personal level? Jesus tells us in John 15:11, when He says,

"These things I have spoken to you, that My joy may remain in you, and that your joy may be full."

It's God's joy in us that allows us to experience the fullness of joy ourselves. In other words, true joy, complete joy, can only be found in a relationship with Jesus Christ. He is the source that never runs out, and as we abide with Him, His joy flows into (and out from) our lives.

Of course, the challenge with joy as an emotion is that hard times often drive our joy away. Jesus is offering us more than the emotion of joy; He is offering us the *mindset* of joy. A mindset is a state of mind, which means it can remain steady despite the volatile experiences of life.

Go back to the word "remain" in John 15:11. The Greek

word is *meno* and it can also be translated "to stay, to endure, to exist permanently." In other words, a mindset, not just an emotion. God's joy can exist permanently in us!

And notice in verse 11 that He wants our joy to be "full." That is the Greek word *pleroo* and it means "to fully, completely fill." So God offers us a complete and permanent filling of His joy!

The key, however, is that we must be connected to Jesus. King David, who knew what it was like to both walk with God and walk away from God, reminds us in Psalm 16:11,

"In Your presence is fullness of joy; at Your right hand are pleasures forevermore."

Let those words sink in. In His presence is fullness of joy, so outside His presence there isn't fullness of joy. This verse speaks of proximity. In order to experience the fullness of joy that Christ purchased for us on the cross, we must enter and pursue an abiding relationship with Him.

The Most Joyful People on the Planet

We, as Christians, should be the most joyful people on the planet! Of course, this does not mean we never experience sadness, frustration, or even disappointment, but as believers we can choose to never camp out in those dark places of the mind because we have a lasting joy that is a result of our salvation in Christ. This is why Jesus said in John 16:33,

"In the world you will have tribulation; but be of good cheer, I have overcome the world."

There are two promises in that verse. First the bad news…we "will" experience tribulation in this world. As we know, Christians are not spared from pain and suffering. Now the good news that swallows up the bad…Jesus has overcome the world! How did Jesus overcome the world? Christ overcame the world by humbling Himself on the cross. Therefore, be of good cheer and be full of unadulterated joy and hope! Thanks to what Jesus accomplished on the cross, our best days, our most joyful days, are still to come. That's what I call great news!

Since Jesus overcame the world, we too, can overcome the world through Him. Just as He overcame through suffering, we also have the power to overcome suffering with His helpful hand. And not just overcome by the skin of our teeth or by a thread, as those sayings go, but valiantly overcome! In fact, as we're about to see in the upcoming chapters, we can experience joy in suffering, and even learn something valuable along the way. But first, let's address why God even allows suffering in the first place.

7

Why Does God Allow Suffering?

As a pastor, student of God's Word, and a fellow human being, I have been asked this question countless times, and of course, I have asked it myself. Thousands of books and sermons have attempted to answer this question, but there is really only one book that's needed—the Bible. The full answer spans from the front cover to the back. On one hand it's a simple answer, on the other it's complex.

But before we dig in, I want to preface my humble attempt to answer this question with three thoughts.

First, I want to assure you this is a very common and normal question, one which every believer wrestles with at one time or another. If you're struggling with this question at this very moment, let me encourage you that you are not alone and there is nothing wrong with you.

Second, this is also a question that has been debated for thousands of years and has been addressed extensively in both literature and oration, so please accept my humble offering as insufficient at best.

Lastly, let me be honest with you up front that the answer to this question doesn't take away any of the pain, but it does place our pain in perspective.

God Created a Perfect World Without Suffering or Death

The Bible teaches that the world was created by God in a perfect state, without war, death, murder, sickness, and suffering. We're told in Genesis 1:31,

"Then God saw everything that He had made, and indeed it was very good."

And at the pinnacle of God's creation was mankind, with the highest level of consciousness, creativity, and will. Genesis 1:27-28 states,

"So God created man in His own image; in the image of God He created him; male and female He created them. Then God blessed them, and God said to them, 'Be fruitful and multiply; fill the earth and subdue it; have dominion over the fish of the sea, over the birds of the air, and over every living thing that moves on the earth.'"

So God created mankind to be an eternal being, similar to Him, and bestowed a sliver of His authority on mankind by entrusting us with the stewardship of His creation. In other words, we were never created to die, but to live in eternal fellowship with God and to enjoy living in harmony with Him and His creation.

Mankind Was Given a Choice

However, for that fellowship to be genuine, a choice had to be given. So God gave mankind the freedom of choice, and along with the power of choice came the responsibility for the consequence, which God clearly laid out in Genesis 2:16-17, when He said,

"Of every tree of the garden you may freely eat; but of the tree of the knowledge of good and evil you shall not eat, for in the day that you eat of it you shall surely die."

Notice, the choice between life and death was given to mankind, and according to Genesis chapter 3, mankind willfully *chose* to disobey God and *knowingly* accepted the consequence—death.

Suffering and Death Entered the Picture

The result was the curse of death, both physically and spiritually. Romans 3:23 tells us,

"For all have sinned and fall short of the glory of God."

Furthermore, Romans 6:23 says,

"For the wages of sin is death."

And so we live in a broken, fallen world that is under the curse of sin, and even now mankind still has free will. We collectively still *choose* to go to war, and murder, and mistreat others, along with countless other horrific acts. But those are not caused by God, none of this was caused by God, from the very beginning it has been caused by man.

Hitting the Reset Button

And so to save us, God sacrificed Himself through Jesus Christ, so that we could live. Jesus said in John 11:25,

[73]

"I am the resurrection and the life. He who believes in Me, though he may die, he shall live."

This is the very reason that Jesus came to 1) redeem the world, and one day in the future 2) judge the world because some will *still* choose *not* to believe.

As the saying goes, the apple doesn't fall far from the tree, and so as descendants of Adam, some still continue to rebel and disobey. But for those who choose life, heaven awaits.

Heaven will be a reset button, where once again His creation will be perfect, but our choice will have already been made (in this lifetime). That's why we're told in Revelation 21:4,

"And God will wipe away every tear from their eyes; there shall be no more death, nor sorrow, nor crying. There shall be no more pain, for the former things have passed away."

> *Suffering doesn't prove God doesn't exist, it only proves how wicked man's heart is*

The topic of how God redeems our suffering and uses it for His glory and our growth will be addressed in the coming chapters. For now, just remember, suffering doesn't prove God doesn't exist, it only proves how wicked man's heart is.

The important things to understand is that God is not the

cause of evil, and He is not apathetic to our suffering. He will one day remove suffering out of the equation, but when that happens, free will is also removed out of the equation. Some may ask why He is taking so long? The answer is in First Peter 3:9,

"The Lord is not slack concerning His promise, as some count slackness, but is longsuffering toward us, not willing that any should perish but that all should come to repentance."

For the time being, free will has been given to each human being to make a choice whether or not they want to have a relationship with God. And no matter how you cut it, you can't have a choice, without also having the option to choose either good or evil.

I can't wait for the "former" things, like suffering and death, to be done away with once and for all. How about you?

8

Can There Be Joy in Trials?

Let's face it, on the surface the idea of joy in trials sounds ridiculous. The very words feel like a contradiction in terms. But that is only if we consider those words in the context of a temporal, earthly perspective. From the perspective of heaven, the view is quite different, and joy in trials makes sense. Remember, as we saw in the previous chapter, trials are unfortunately part of life for the time being. If we were unable to experience joy in trials, then we would be unable to experience joy...because life is *always* full of trials!

As Christians, we have the capacity through the power of the Holy Spirit to understand there is a bigger picture, a larger narrative taking place, beyond each moment that we live. We may physically exist at a defined moment in time and space, but our understanding has the ability to transcend both. So we can experience joy in trials, not because trials bring joy, but because we know more is taking place beyond the trial itself.

Remember in Chapter 3, the illustration of the planet spinning at 1,000 miles per hour that we don't feel? God is always working, and because God is good and He loves us, we know that He's doing good in and through our lives, despite the trial.

This is why Paul wrote, in Romans 8:28,

"And we know that all things work together for good to those who love God, to those who are the called according to His purpose."

The phrase "all things" is pretty definitive. Of course, this doesn't mean that bad circumstances are good. It can't be logically argued that losing a job, going bankrupt, or suffering a debilitating disease are good things—they're not. But as followers of God, He will work those things together for our good. Something good will come from the bad, a miraculous working that only God could accomplish! That's the big picture. That's an eternal-minded perspective. Which is why joy in trials, if you look at those words from a biblical viewpoint, are not a contradiction at all.

Pre-ordering a Dose of Joy

Have you ever pre-ordered a book, movie, album, or video game? Maybe you planned a wedding or booked a vacation a year in advance? In that moment you experienced joy and excitement, based on a *future* benefit. You weren't wiggling your toes in the sandy beaches of Hawaii just yet, but simply knowing that you would be, someday soon, gave you a little spring in your step in the present moment. And that's just the emotion of joy; imagine what life would be like with a mindset of joy?

In many ways, experiencing joy in trials is possible because we can celebrate the future good that God is working, even during the present suffering. That's what

Jesus did, when we read in Hebrews 12:2.

"Who for the joy that was set before Him endured the cross, despising the shame, and has sat down at the right hand of the throne of God."

The cross wasn't fun for Jesus. He was fully God, but also fully human, yet without sin. I'm sure that fully human part was not eager to experience the suffering and pain of the cross. This is likely what Jesus meant when He said, in the Garden of Gethsemane,

"O My Father, if it is possible, let this cup [of suffering] *pass from Me; nevertheless, not as I will, but as You will"* *(Matthew 26:39)*

> *Jesus was not looking forward to the cross, He was looking beyond the cross to the joy that would come through it*

What is Jesus saying here? He's saying that He will submit to the Father and stick with the plan, but if there's any other way to accomplish the mission, if it's possible, let's go that direction instead! Jesus was not looking forward to the cross, He was looking beyond the cross to the joy that would come through it.

We can do the same thing. We can choose to look past the suffering, past the trial, to endure our cross like Jesus did, as we focus instead on the joy set before us.

Okay, Here's the Bad News (or Maybe It's Good News?)

Some may be thinking, cool, I'm willing to pre-order a dose of joy when I have to, and I fully accept why there is suffering in this cursed world; I even understand why Jesus had to endure the cross to pay a debt I was unable to pay, but why do *I* have to suffer? Everything is acceptable theoretically, until it hits home personally.

In James 1:2-4, he kind of sneaks a fast one in there, when he writes those immortal words,

"My brethren, count it all joy when you fall into various trials, knowing that the testing of your faith produces patience. But let patience have its perfect work, that you may be perfect and complete, lacking nothing."

There's so much powerful truth packed into those words that it's very easy to miss the word "when." James says "when you fall" into trials, not "if." In other words, trials are an inevitable guarantee, whether we like it or not, whether we think we deserve it or not.

We can even take it back a step and consider *who* James is writing to when he says, "My brethren." Who are his brethren? He is referring to believers, fellow bondservants of Jesus Christ.

There are false doctrines floating around out there today that claim true Christians should never suffer trials or hardship. They wrongly assert that as children of God, He owes us the good life, living on easy street in this world with big houses, fancy cars, and plenty of money to burn. Therefore, their erroneous conclusion is that *all* suffering or difficulty in your life is the result of your own sin, lack of faith, or false conversion. Let me tell you right now that the Bible clearly teaches the exact opposite.

Of course, every false doctrine must have an element of truth to make it believable, so let's consider these points before going further, in order to avoid any misunderstanding.

Are there Christians who God has materialistically blessed, and even those who "appear" to experience minimal hardship (I say "appear" because no one truly knows what it's like to hurt in someone else's shoes—just because the grass may "appear" greener doesn't mean it is)? Yes. Is that wrong? Of course not; He's God and every resource in the universe is His, so He may distribute them as He sovereignly wills. But does He *owe* us material excess, or a life free from hardship? No, that's the error of the false doctrine.

Regarding suffering, is it true that our own sin or lack of faith can produce difficulty in our lives? Absolutely. If my lack of faith leads me to decide I'm going to take matters into my own hands by robbing a bank, which leads to my arrest and imprisonment, that is clearly my own fault. But a car rear-ending me at a stoplight on my way to church is not the result of my sin or lack of faith. Both scenarios resulted in hardship, but by two different causes. So is all suffering the result of the failure of a believer? Not at all.

This is why it is so important that we read our Bibles and understand what God is teaching us through His written

Word. Looking to God for answers clears up so much misunderstanding and confusion. So what does the Bible tell us about the suffering of the believer?

Peter, a disciple of Jesus, much acquainted with pain and suffering (church tradition tells us he too was crucified, except upside down), tells us,

"For to this you were called, because Christ also suffered for us, leaving us an example, that you should follow His steps" (First Peter 2:21).

Furthermore, Peter goes on to write,

"Beloved, do not think it strange concerning the fiery trial which is to try you, as though some strange thing happened to you; but rejoice to the extent that you partake of Christ's sufferings, that when His glory is revealed, you may also be glad with exceeding joy" (First Peter 4:12-13).

So here's the bad news: we are called to suffer. Suffering is actually part of the calling of being a follower of Jesus. Peter even goes so far as to say we shouldn't think "some strange thing happened" when we experience a fiery trial. Peter is giving us a heads up that even with mountain-moving faith, trials are still part of the universal package.

The biblical doctrine of suffering continues to be solidified by Jesus' own words of suffering in John 15:18,

"If the world hates you, you know that it hated Me before it hated you."

Jesus knows firsthand the effects of sin on this world and

He allowed Himself to be fully immersed in the awful experience. He did not spare Himself the pain, but lived out trials of rejection, death of loved ones, poverty, hunger, physical suffering—ultimately even spiritual separation from the Father as the result of our sin.

The prophet Isaiah described Christ's experience for us in gruesome, vivid detail,

"He is despised and rejected by men, a Man of sorrows and acquainted with grief…Surely He has borne our griefs and carried our sorrows; yet we esteemed Him stricken, smitten by God, and afflicted. But He was wounded for our transgressions, He was bruised for our iniquities…He was oppressed and He was afflicted, yet He opened not His mouth; He was led as a lamb to the slaughter" (Isaiah 53:3-5, 7).

Here's where this all comes together because Jesus declares, in Matthew 10:24,

"A disciple is not above his teacher, nor a servant above his master."

So, if Jesus suffered in life, and He's our master, then why would we think we wouldn't suffer also?

But there's a silver lining (several, actually)!

First, since Jesus, our Lord and Savior, is no stranger to human suffering, this means we are not alone in our experience because He's right there with us—and He *understands*. Jesus is not aloof and preoccupied, disengaged and missing from the action; He's right there, in the storm, in the fire, walking by our side. He doesn't sleep, or have to go home, or have to divide His attention; He is with us through *every* ordeal, the good and the bad, that life throws our way.

> *Jesus is not aloof and preoccupied, disengaged and missing from the action; He's right there, in the storm, in the fire, walking by our side*

Second, because Jesus has experienced the full gamut of human pain, He truly is the best qualified to lead us through our own suffering, giving us, as Peter stated, "an example, that [we] should follow His steps." The fulfillment of Isaiah's messianic prophecies is documented in the Gospels, where we can learn from Jesus' response to the suffering He endured.

Third, as Peter pointed out, when we suffer, we can rejoice to the extent that we "partake of Christ's sufferings," which means through the fellowship of trials, we become closer to God. Like soldiers in the trenches of war, or a team slogging through a championship season, the shared experience of battle and hardship draws and binds people together. We don't fully experience Christ's sufferings, as Peter points out, we only "partake" to an "extent," but it's enough to create a closer intimacy, unity, and oneness with Him.

Fourth, when Jesus returns fully in glory, because He endured and overcame the cross, we too will be "glad with exceeding joy" because His glory is our victory as well!

So you see, even though on one hand we may feel that our calling to suffer like Christ is a privilege we'd rather skip, the reality is that hardship brings many layers of blessings, and that *is* cause for joy!

Nothing Goes to Waste

One of the great manifestations of God's love and grace toward us is that He redeems our trials and tribulations, ensuring they aren't pointless experiences. Nothing with God is without purpose. Remember, God doesn't enjoy watching us hurt, so He uses our hurt to bring about a spiritual work in our lives. He loves us so much He doesn't let our suffering go to waste.

That is why in James 1:2, we're encouraged to "count it all joy" when we have trials in life. Trials inevitably bring about a spiritual work in us.

What is that spiritual work? In verse 3, James tells us, "the testing of your faith produces patience."

The Greek word used for patience in this verse is *hupomone*, which means "endurance" or "constancy." This word alludes to more than just bearing some annoying or irritating affliction. It speaks to a state of standing fast, to outlasting, to enduring, and to turning adversities into opportunities.

In 2006, the last movie of the Rocky franchise came out, titled, *Rocky Balboa*. In the movie, Rocky is now a retired professional boxer, who owns and runs a restaurant. His son is now an adult who's grown up bitter about living under his dad's shadow. In one particularly memorable scene, Rocky's son lays into his dad outside the restaurant, whining and complaining about how hard his life has been.

In response, Rocky, the champion boxer who has overcome adversity over and over again, offers these great lines, "The world ain't all sunshine and rainbows. It's a very mean and nasty place and I don't care how tough you are it will beat you to your knees and keep you there permanently if you let it. You, me, or nobody is gonna hit as hard as life. But it ain't about how hard ya hit. It's about how hard you can get hit and keep moving forward. How much you can take and keep moving forward. That's how winning is done!"

That quote always makes me think of *hupomone*, the lasting patience and endurance James is speaking of. When our faith is tested by hard times, God redeems it by producing in us the ability to endure, to keep moving forward. This is how when the entire world is falling apart, we can remain steadfast and strong in Jesus Christ. James is telling us that the testing of our faith makes us stronger.

Have you ever done strength training, or cardio exercises like running, cycling, or swimming? The physical resistance of weight, gravity, or water against our body hurts; it's uncomfortable, even a little painful. So why do we continue to do it? Because we know that resistance builds strength. It hurts when we push back against the object of resistance, but it also makes us stronger. Over time we can lift more weight, run farther, and swim longer as a result. In a physical sense, the testing of the body produces endurance. Likewise, but on a much grander scale, through the strength and power of Jesus Christ working in our lives, we can push back against the adversities of life, knowing that we will gain the endurance to keep moving forward.

And for what purpose does God want us to keep moving forward? According to James 1:4,

"But let patience [hupomone/endurance] *have its perfect work, that you may be perfect and complete, lacking nothing."*

When it comes to trials and sufferings, God's end goal is our perfection, our completeness. In other words, God redeems all the hardship we go through to bring about the finished masterpiece in each of our lives.

Is it painful? It often is, but God is not causing the pain, He is redeeming it. When our faith is tested through the fire of hardship, the experience is not inherently joyful. However, if we can remember that God will use the pain to bring about perfection and completeness in our lives, then we can *choose* to find the joy in the trial.

9

Changing Our Mindset

We've seen that a mindset of joy begins with first having a relationship with God, the source of all joy. It's His joy in us that allows us to transcend fleeting emotions, and instead walk in a steady attitude of joyfulness. Knowing Him, and knowing who we are called to be in Him, as a result of the cross, is a game-changer! Still, like Rocky said, life has a tendency to beat us down to our knees. So God redeems our suffering and restores our joy, by using trials and tribulations to draw us closer in intimacy to Him, to build an enduring faith in us, and to mature us so that we are "perfect and complete, lacking nothing."

> *A thankful person is a joyful person, and a joyful person is a thankful person—they go hand in hand*

God doesn't force anything on us. We still, even now, operate in a balance of our free will and God's sovereignty. This means it's still our individual choice whether we will choose a mindset of joy. But do you see how God has given us an overwhelming number of reasons to be joyful?

Especially when you combine the biblical reasons for being thankful *and* being joyful.

The choice is ours, but God has made sure to give us every reason to choose properly. He has accomplished this by giving us everything we need. We're reminded in Second Peter 1:3,

"His divine power has given to us all things that pertain to life and godliness, through the knowledge of Him who called us by glory and virtue."

And in Philippians 4:19, Paul begins to wrap up his letter with these words,

"And my God shall supply all your need according to His riches in glory by Christ Jesus."

This means, in the context of joy, that we have everything we need to be thankful and joyful. In fact, a heart of thankfulness and a mindset of joy actually feed into one another. A thankful person is a joyful person, and a joyful person is a thankful person—they go hand in hand!

We're not done yet though. God gives us instructions on how we can change our mindset, to help us think clearly, so we can choose to be joyful.

1. Ask in Faith for Wisdom

There are many scriptures that we use the general principle in broad application, but the actual context of the verses that precede and follow a specific verse is vitally important. James 1:5-8 is a perfect example. This particular text is a powerful statement on wisdom and faith, but what many forget in the broad application of these truths is it is within the context of speaking of trials and tribulations, that James writes,

"If any of you lacks wisdom, let him ask of God, who gives to all liberally and without reproach, and it will be given to him. But let him ask in faith, with no doubting, for he who doubts is like a wave of the sea driven and tossed by the wind. For let not that man suppose that he will receive anything from the Lord; he is a double-minded man, unstable in all his ways."

So these truths about wisdom and faith are specifically in reference to trials and tribulations. I think we can all agree that wisdom would be a very helpful tool to draw upon as we go through life's trials. So what is this biblical wisdom that James speaks of?

The book of Proverbs, most popularly known as the book of wisdom, translates the word "wisdom" from the Hebrew word *chokmah*, which means "skillful." Biblical wisdom is living life skillfully. Or, another way of saying it is, having the skills to live life well. We need this ability when we're going through challenging times.

The best part is we don't have to go on a treasure hunt to find wisdom for ourselves. God offers to give it to us! All we have to do is ask. Verse 5 clearly states He will give it "liberally and without reproach," meaning that God won't hold anything back, and He won't shame us for asking.

It's interesting how God covers all the bases here. Often, what prevents people from asking for help is a fear their request will be rejected, or that they will be looked down upon for asking. The Lord addresses both these fears by promising to answer our request for wisdom by giving it generously and without recrimination.

However, there is a part we have to play in the balance between man's responsibility and God's sovereignty. We must "ask in faith, with no doubting" (James 1:6).

Putting Our Faith Where Our Mouth Is

You may have heard the story of the Great Blondin, who was like the Evel Knievel of the 1800s. He once strung a tightrope across Niagara Falls and asked the crowd who gathered around if they believed he could cross it.

Of course, they enthusiastically replied, "We believe! We believe!"

So he walked across the thin rope and came back again. Amidst their applause and cheering, he asked, "How many of you believe that I, the Great Blondin, can not only walk back across the tightrope, but this time do it while I push a wheelbarrow?"

"We believe!" they yelled louder, wanting to see him accomplish the seemingly impossible.

He then challenged his crowd, asking, "How many of you *really* believe?"

"Oh, we really believe it!" they shouted back to him.

There was one man in particular who was yelling a little bit louder than the rest of the crowd, so the Great Blondin pointed to him and said, "Get in the wheelbarrow." Petrified, the man quickly disappeared!

If we ask God for wisdom, yet doubt He will give it to us, we are like a "wave of the sea driven and tossed by the wind." Not only that, but verses 7 and 8 read, "For let not that man suppose that he will receive anything from the Lord; he is a double-minded man, unstable in all his ways."

If this sounds harsh, we must remember that faith is a vital component in our walk with Jesus. So much so that Hebrews 11:6 tells us,

"But without faith it is impossible to please Him, for he who comes to God must believe that He is, and that He is a rewarder of those who diligently seek Him."

Faith is not an optional ingredient in the recipe, it's mandatory. It's impossible to fully please God without faith. This is why Jesus tells us in Matthew 7:7-8,

"Ask, and it will be given to you; seek, and you will find; knock, and it will be opened to you. For everyone who asks receives, and he who seeks finds, and to him who knocks it will be opened."

God doesn't need our help, but He wants our involvement. He wants us to "get in the wheelbarrow." We don't have to walk across the tightrope—He is the miracle worker, not us—but we do have to be willing to step out in faith.

Praying According to His Will

Hear me in this—when we pray, if we're praying according to God's will, then we need to pray with confidence and assurance that the prayer request will be answered. The key is praying according to *His* will, not ours.

Let me give you a personal example from my life. Whenever I teach a message, I pray to God that He will give me the right words to speak. I pray to be led by the Spirit and not by my flesh. I base my prayer on First Peter 4:11, which says,

"If anyone speaks, let him speak as the oracles of God."

Scripture tells me that when I teach, I need to take it seriously. I cannot be dismissive, nonchalant, lazy, or cavalier about this responsibility. So when I pray, I ask God to speak through me as I teach. I know with certainty that I'm asking according to His will because the Bible calls us to reverence in teaching God's Word; therefore, I can pray with confidence that He will answer my prayer.

> If God wants us to pray for wisdom, then we can pray with bold assurance that He will give us the wisdom we seek— there literally is no reason for us to doubt

God promises to give us wisdom, or the skills to live life well, "liberally and without reproach." In other words, it is God's will, His desire, for us to ask for wisdom. And if God wants us to pray for wisdom, then we can pray with bold assurance that He will give us the wisdom we seek—there literally is no reason for us to doubt.

2. Spend Time at the Feet of Jesus

Too often we get lost in our own heads because we get preoccupied thinking about ourselves. We start to compare and contrast, and joy begins to quickly fade. However, nothing restores a mindset of joy better than reorienting our thinking by shifting our focus away from ourselves and back onto Jesus.

In Luke 10:38-42, we see this scenario play out with the sisters, Mary and Martha. Jesus was visiting their home and as He spoke, Mary was sitting at His feet and listening, probably hanging on every word that came out of His mouth. But Martha was focused on being a hostess and serving everybody, so she got frustrated that her sister, Mary, wasn't helping. So Martha complained to Jesus, soliciting His assistance to get Mary off the floor to help her.

Jesus responds with these words in verses 41-42,

"Martha, Martha, you are worried and troubled about many things. But one thing is needed, and Mary has chosen that good part, which will not be taken away from her."

Apparently, Martha had a lot of stuff on her mind, much more than simply playing hostess to Jesus' home visit. He said she was "worried and troubled about many things." And then He gives Martha the answer to her unrest. Jesus says that "one thing is needed" for a troubled mind like Martha's, and ironically, Mary is the one doing it! What was Mary doing? She was spending time with Jesus, resting in Him, and learning from Him. The answer to a troubled mind is not to distract ourselves with busy work, the answer is to spend time at the feet of Jesus.

Check out Jesus' words in Matthew 11:28-30,

"Come to Me, all you who labor and are heavy laden, and I will give you rest. Take My yoke upon you and learn from Me, for I am gentle and lowly in heart, and you will find rest for your souls. For My yoke is easy and My burden is light."

Do you feel Christ's yoke is easy and His burden is light? Do you regularly "find rest" for your soul? I'll be honest with you, there are many times I feel the exact opposite. So if there's a disconnect between what Jesus says and what we feel, then there are really only two options: either He is wrong, or we are. Obviously, Jesus can't be wrong, so what are we doing wrong? Go back to the key opening statement in verse 28 that starts it all—"Come to Me."

Mary was answering that call, but Martha was distracting herself with being busy. Mary was focused on Jesus, Martha was focused on life's problems. Mary was resting in Christ, Martha was stressed out and freaking out.

The contrast is clear and as Jesus said, Mary chose the "good part" between the two. The same is true for us. We have a choice in where we place the focus of our minds. One direction will rob us of joy, the other will only increase it.

David proclaimed in Psalm 16:11,

"In Your presence is fullness of joy; at Your right hand are pleasures forevermore."

In God's presence is fullness of joy! There's nowhere else we will find a sustaining joy. It can only be found in Jesus.

To experience a mindset of joy in the midst of trials and tribulations is a choice that each of us must make, but if we 1) ask in faith for God to give us the wisdom we need to navigate life's troubled waters, and 2) spend time resting at Jesus' feet where we can focus on Him and not the problems around us, then we will transform our thinking and open the door to a mindset of joy!

Part Three:

Choosing a Position of Victory

10

Are We Warriors or Weaklings?

In the movie, *The Usual Suspects*, there is a great line that states, "The greatest trick the devil ever pulled was convincing the world he didn't exist." There is truth in that statement. Satan can't change reality, so he likes to turn reality on its head.

For example, Jesus completed the redemptive work of the cross. That's why He said in John 19:30,

"'It is finished!' And bowing His head, He gave up His spirit."

The mission was accomplished. Jesus had completed what He'd been sent to earth to do—to redeem mankind.

Satan cannot change this reality. He can't undo the finished work of the cross. So he does the next best thing that *is* within his power—like the quote from *The Usual Suspects*, he convinces the world the cross didn't exist. Or, in the case of the life of the believer, to *forget* that it did.

Open Prison Doors, Set the Captives Free

Imagine a prisoner sitting in their cell. It's dark, cramped, and dirty...but the door is wide open! At any moment, all they need to do is get up off their bunk and walk out. Except they don't. Instead, they choose to stay in the cell, even while freedom is on the other side of the door.

Essentially, this is what Satan tries to do in the life of the believer because he can't change reality.

The prophet Isaiah, in speaking of the future Messiah, 700 years before Jesus was born, proclaimed,

"He has sent Me to heal the brokenhearted, to proclaim liberty to the captives, and the opening of the prison to those who are bound" (Isaiah 61:1).

Then, in Luke 4:16-21, Jesus said He fulfilled the prophecy of Isaiah 61, when He stated in verse 21,

"Today this Scripture is fulfilled in your hearing."

The reality is that we are prisoners who have been set free! The prison door has been flung open by the victory of Jesus Christ. We are no longer imprisoned by our sinful impulses, feelings of hopelessness, and a lack of true meaning in life.

Satan can't reverse this victory, but he can tempt us to forget. He can distract us with the familiarity of the prison cell, so that though we are free, we choose to remain in the cell, not experiencing the power and victory that Jesus secured for us on the cross.

If we don't exercise our freedom, and instead voluntarily remain imprisoned, then it's almost like negating the power of the cross in our individual lives, without actually undoing the work. It's the elephant being afraid of the mouse, a total role-reversal perpetuated by our enemy. It's clever, it's manipulative, and it's 100% avoidable by the believer.

God's Word tells us that we are victors not victims, warriors not wimps, and conquerors not the conquered

---

So once again, walking in a position of victory comes down to the battle of the mind, and making an important choice that no one can make for us. God's Word tells us that we are victors not victims, warriors not weaklings, and conquerors not the conquered.

Being a Super-Conqueror

Paul tells us in Romans 8:35 and 37,

"Who shall separate us from the love of Christ? Shall tribulation, or distress, or persecution, or famine, or nakedness, or peril, or sword? Yet in all these things we are more than conquerors through Him who loved us."

There is so much truth packed into those verses.

First, notice that there is a lot of adversity and suffering packed into verse 35, from distress to peril. Again, Paul is writing to Christians. We are not exempt from the struggles of this world; however, as we're going to see next, we have an advantage the world doesn't have.

Second, despite those hardships, the Bible says we are

"more than conquerors." You may wonder how someone can be *more* than a conqueror? After all, isn't a conqueror a conqueror? On the field of battle, you either win or lose, there isn't more than a winner.

The Greek word *hupernikao* is used here and it means "to vanquish beyond, to gain a decisive victory." My favorite football team is the New England Patriots. I watched them play the Chargers the other day. Technically, a team only needs to win the game by one point more than the other to be victorious. In this particular game, the Patriots beat the Chargers, 45 to 0. There's winning and then there's *winning*. We're not just conquerors, we're *super*-conquerors! That's the emphasis Paul is making.

Third, it's "through Him who loved us," Jesus, that this is all possible. It's not because of us. Independent of God, we are not powerful. It is His power, His Spirit in us, that makes our position of victory a reality.

Paul wrote to his protégé Timothy, in Second Timothy 1:7,

"For God has not given us a spirit of fear, but of power and of love and of a sound mind."

The word for power is the Greek word *dunamis*. It's where we derive our English words, dynamite and dynamic. It is used to describe the very power of God, and Paul is telling Timothy (and us) that God has *given* us that same spirit of power.

We didn't earn it, we can't deserve it, it is completely unmerited. Like everything else God gives us, it is simply a gift of grace. We have the power of God in us. We are therefore super-conquerors in Him.

It is this reality that Satan wishes we would neglect, ignore, and forget because it is advantageous to him for us to do so. Yet for us, remembering our position of victory and walking in it is the difference between victorious living or living in defeat.

When we claim the position of victory that Jesus purchased for us on the cross, we can say, as Paul said in Second Corinthians 4:8-9,

"We are hard-pressed on every side, yet not crushed; we are perplexed, but not in despair; persecuted, but not forsaken; struck down, but not destroyed."

Don't let Satan convince you he has the upper hand—he doesn't. He's a bully on the playground of life, plain and simple, but he's no match for the God who has our back.

If we stand on the promises of who we are in Christ, and who our God is, then we will be well equipped to remember our position of victory. And that position is key when it comes to facing the double-whammy of trials and temptation that life inevitably brings.

11

Do Trials and Temptation Go Hand in Hand?

On a certain level, it may initially appear that walking victoriously through trials has nothing to do with overcoming temptation in our lives. However, consider that most of the greatest errors we make in life occur in an environment of pain and desperation. Feelings of marital neglect may lead to adultery, financial stress may lead to theft, and the list goes on and on.

Granted, the frustrations and difficulties we experience in life are no excuse for us to rebel against God's will, but that is often how it begins. Feelings of powerlessness, insecurity, and fear make us vulnerable to the enemy's deceptions.

That's why it's imperative we overcome temptation, especially when it coincides with the vulnerability we feel in times of suffering. But first, we must understand why trials and temptation often go hand in hand.

Flipsides of the Same Coin

Let's go back to the book of James for a moment. Just a handful of verses following his exhortation to choose joy in times of trials, we are reminded in James 1:12,

"Blessed is the man who endures temptation; for when he has been approved, he will receive the crown of life which the Lord has promised to those who love Him."

As further evidence that trials and temptation often go hand in hand, the Greek word for temptation here in verse 12 is *peirasmos*, which is the exact same word used for "trials" in James 1:2.

James isn't talking about two separate things; he's actually talking about the same thing. Think of it like this. I'm sure we would all agree that trials are a temptation, and temptations most certainly are trials in our lives.

When we go through trials, when we have moments where we feel weary or discouraged or beaten down—let's face it, after all, we're still human—that's when temptation to sin often presents itself. This is especially true when we stop seeing ourselves as God sees us (victorious children of the King) and instead begin to see ourselves the way the world sees us (pathetic, helpless, and weak).

Adventures in Law Enforcement

Years ago, I owned my own property management business, and believe me when I say it was tough being in real estate during the Great Recession. After a while all I wanted to do was get out of that business. I wanted a new career.

Now don't ask me why, but I figured the most logical thing to do would be to apply for the sheriff's department, so I did.

I remember the recruiting officer was all fired up about me. It was actually kind of scary. He told me I was going to be in the Academy within two weeks. That's how quickly the process was moving along. Everything seemed to be on a fast track. I passed the written test. I passed the physical agility test. I passed the interview. I even passed the polygraph with flying colors.

As I said, all this happened in a very short period of time, but when I submitted my background check packet, all of a sudden things came to a grinding halt. Then, at the end of six months, I got a denial letter informing me I was no longer in consideration to be a deputy.

I was so confused. I couldn't imagine anyone that I listed on the background check saying anything bad about me that would have derailed the entire process. I had disclosed everything to them, and I do mean *everything*. So much so that the recruiting officer and the polygraph examiner actually laughed when I told them about the worst things I've ever done. They found it funny! Naturally, I was stunned and confused at what possibly could have disqualified me.

So I shared the news with a friend from church who was a deputy sheriff at the same department I had applied to. Due to his experience, he was actually walking through the whole process with me. He had known that things were initially happening really fast, then dramatically slowed down, now culminating in the rejection letter.

The first thing he asked me was how were my finances? Remember, my business was in real estate during the recession, so my financial situation was pretty lousy.

When you have no money and you have to put gas in the car, you put it on the credit card; when you need to get groceries to feed the family, you put it on the credit card. I knew that was not a wise thing to do, but I really didn't have a choice. As a result, I had collected quite a bit of debt. I also had some late payments, and a few of those I had actually fallen pretty far behind in.

My buddy told me my negative financial situation was probably the reason they disqualified me. In fact, he said after going so far successfully into the process, that was actually the most common reason why somebody would be disqualified.

Here's the logic, as he explained it. As a deputy they knew I would have access to money when I arrested someone, or when I searched a home or a vehicle. The risk of a deputy who was struggling financially and having access to easy money was too much of a chance for temptation in their eyes. So much of a temptation, it would seem, that enough law enforcement officers had already been in sufficient trouble with this issue in the past, that I wasn't worth taking a chance on.

Trials and temptations are flipsides of the same coin. Apparently even the sheriff's department thinks so!

This may seem like more bad news, but fortunately, as we have already seen in the previous two sections of this book, God always overshadows the bad news with great news, worthy of our thankfulness and joy, and it's all right there in verse 12.

Overcoming Brings Happiness

For a follower of Jesus Christ, happiness is not a destination unto itself, but rather a byproduct along the journey of building an abiding relationship with God. On that journey of growing closer to Jesus and conforming more and more to His image, we too must confront and overcome temptation, just as He did. When we do, we will experience the promise of James 1:12, which says, "Blessed is the man who endures temptation."

> *Happiness is not a destination unto itself, but rather a byproduct along the journey of building an abiding relationship with God*

This touches on a familiar theme of joy in trials. That word "blessed" is very interesting. In Greek it's the word *makarios*, which means "happy" and "fortunate." The Bible is telling us that it's a joyful experience when we persevere, when we are victorious over temptation.

Have you ever persevered over a trial or a temptation? Isn't it a great feeling to walk in a position of victory?

I remember when I was a young adult I had quite a temper

behind the wheel of a vehicle. I've shouted mean things out the window, thrown objects at vehicles, and chased people on (and off) the freeway. I had a serious anger problem.

I'll never forget the moment, many, many years ago, when someone actually had the audacity to both cut me off and give me the finger at the same time. I just shrugged it off and kept driving. Nothing stirred up in me; I was at peace. I didn't feel it was necessary to get angry and chase the offender down, but trust me when I say in my youth that's exactly what I would've done. I remember in that moment actually being surprised by my lack of a reaction.

What happened to me? Jesus happened to me! He had changed me and given me victory over an area of sin. It is an amazing feeling of triumph in Christ to successfully endure temptation, to turn it down and walk away. It is certainly cause for joy and celebration, and feeling blessed.

There is another reason why James tells us we are blessed.

You Can't Beat a Heavenly Reward

No one can outgive God. Verse 12 continues, "for when he has been approved, he will receive the crown of life which the Lord has promised to those who love Him."

Remember, every hardship we experience is redeemed for our spiritual growth. In this life, God is using the circumstances of our lives to bring about a supernatural work to make us more and more like Jesus. As if that weren't amazing enough, the benefits don't end there. He also offers us rewards in heaven. Hebrews 11:6 states,

"He is a rewarder of those who diligently seek Him."

Those who persevere over temptation, those who love Jesus Christ, will receive a reward in heaven for their faithfulness—they will receive the crown of life.

Paul tells us about this crown in First Corinthians 9:24-25, when he writes,

"Do you not know that those who run in a race all run, but one receives the prize? Run in such a way that you may obtain it. And everyone who competes for the prize is temperate in all things. Now they do it to obtain a perishable crown, but we for an imperishable crown."

Not only will God bless us in this life for persevering over the twin challenges of trials and temptation, but He will also reward us in the next life!

So we have seen the blessing, but how exactly do we overcome temptation? Especially the temptation to give into fear, to doubt the goodness of God, to succumb to discouragement and hopelessness, and to view ourselves as less than we really are, along with the host of other temptations that kind of thinking brings? As always, God never calls us to do something without giving us clear instruction on how to get it done.

[114]

12

How Can We Overcome Temptation?

When my younger brother, Eddie, was a teenager, he struggled with alcohol. For a decade of his life he surrendered himself to the control of a bottle. Then one day he had enough and committed his life to Jesus. He traded one addiction for another, and from that point forward he walked in sobriety with Jesus, but he also walked with humble caution.

Eddie was aware of his weakness, so he avoided any environment where alcohol was present. If he inadvertently walked into a room where there were open containers of alcohol, he would turn around and leave.

God honored his faithfulness and humility. Eddie has been sober now for decades, and he is the senior pastor of Calvary Chapel Brazos Valley in Texas, where he serves with his wife, Sheri, and their growing family.

Temptation Exposes Weakness

Temptation in and of itself is not a sin. We know that Jesus was tempted, yet He never sinned. However, temptation is certainly a gateway to sin. Temptation also reveals our inherent weaknesses. What may tempt one person does not necessarily tempt another; only the one who is susceptible is tempted. It's not a coincidence that Satan tempted Jesus with bread after He had been fasting for forty days and nights, and He was hungry. That's the same reason Eddie stayed as far away from alcohol as possible. He knew he had a weakness, and he didn't want to give that weakness any edge over him.

In times of suffering and hardship, the cracks and weaknesses that are already there in our character begin to more easily manifest themselves

In times of suffering and hardship, the cracks and weaknesses that are already there in our character begin to more easily manifest themselves because we are under stress. Our insecurities and fears are harder to cover up, our lack of faith becomes more difficult to conceal, and we find ourselves involuntarily and uncomfortably exposed. We may even discover problem areas of our lives we didn't know existed. We are tempted to behave in ways that are inconsistent with our normal behavior and beliefs.

Suddenly, believers genuinely become fearful the government is going to permanently close down the Church, even though they *know* the Church is not a building, it's a family of believers, and Jesus promised in Matthew 16:18,

"On this rock I will build My church, and the gates of Hades shall not prevail against it."

In the name of allegiance to imperfect politicians or manmade political parties, believers turn against their fellow believers, even though they *know* Paul exhorts,

"With all lowliness and gentleness, with longsuffering, bearing with one another in love, endeavoring to keep the unity of the Spirit in the bond of peace" (Ephesians 4:2-3).

Where does this inconsistent behavior come from? How can we know truth, yet still act on lies?

The reality is we are all susceptible to temptation even on a good day, much less a bad one. Even Paul was able to admit in Romans 7:19 and 24,

"For the good that I will to do, I do not do; but the evil I will not to do, that I practice...O wretched man that I am!"

Times of suffering and hardship only make this struggle worse. That is why it is absolutely necessary for us to know how to overcome temptation, but to do so, we must first understand its origin.

Where Temptation *Doesn't* Come From

When we are hurting, it is so easy to blame God. If it's true that we lash out at those closest to us, then nobody is closer than Him. But just like blaming God for the world's suffering is wrong, He is equally not at fault for our temptations. In fact, James 1:13 clearly states,

"Let no one say when he is tempted, 'I am tempted by God'; for God cannot be tempted by evil, nor does He Himself tempt anyone."

God does not tempt us. It would be a contradiction of His character for Him to call us to walk in victory from sin, while at the same time pointing us to sin.

Now, in His sovereignty, God knows what will happen to us, and again, in His sovereignty, He does allow us to be tempted. God may lead us into situations where our weaknesses and propensities are unearthed, so we can acknowledge and work them out, or even reveal an area of victory (for example, allowing the guy to cut me off on the freeway). Hear me in this—God sovereignly allowing temptation to come does *not* mean He is the one who is tempting us.

Likewise, God cannot be tempted by sin. Satan has no leverage over God because He is perfect and has no weakness. Satan cannot cause God to be less than Himself, or to do anything contradictory to His holy character.

Of course, I did state earlier than Jesus was tempted by Satan when He was hungry. In Matthew 4:1, we read,

"Then Jesus was led up by the Spirit into the wilderness to be tempted by the devil."

If God can't be tempted, then how was Jesus tempted? Remember, Jesus was both fully God and fully man, and therefore, in being fully human, Jesus understands what it's like to be tempted in the flesh, yet without sin. Hebrews 4:15

tells us,

"For we do not have a High Priest who cannot sympathize with our weaknesses, but was in all points tempted as we are, yet without sin."

It is a great encouragement that 1) Jesus can actually sympathize with our struggle against temptation, and 2) that He was an example of victory over temptation. Though we aren't perfect like Jesus, His Spirit does dwell in us, which means we have the power to be victorious over temptation as well!

Jesus knows firsthand what it's like to be tempted, to suffer, and to endure trials. Yet He experienced all those hardships without sin because He is also fully God. Think about that—Jesus can *relate* to us; He *understands* us! I am absolutely blown away by that fact.

Are you amazed that Jesus Christ, the creator of the universe, can look into your life, and it's actually something He can *relate* to? That is so crazy to me! This means Jesus can connect with us on a true level of intimacy and understanding regarding the suffering and hardship we experience in life. Whatever season we go through, we don't go through it alone.

That's the great news! God is on our side and He is walking with us every step of the way. He is not the cause of our suffering or temptation; He is our Savior and the source of our strength, power, and victory.

With the foundation set, we can now begin to lay out a battle plan for overcoming temptation as we choose a position of victory.

1. Realize Temptation Begins Internally, not Externally

If temptation doesn't come from God, so where does it come from? Are you ready to face the uncomfortable truth? According to James 1:14-15,

"But each one is tempted when he is drawn away by his own desires and enticed. Then, when desire has conceived, it gives birth to sin; and sin, when it is full-grown, brings forth death."

According to this scripture, temptation begins with our own desires. The progression here is not coincidental, it's a systematic process. Let's walk through the steps of these verses in chronological order.

First, we are drawn away by our own desires. In Greek, the phrase "drawn away" actually means to be dragged. That sounds scary! So we are dragged away by our own desires. No one is doing this to us. These are sinful desires already within us, but we are allowing them to draw us away.

Then, as we are dragged away, we are enticed. The word for "enticed" in Greek actually means we become entrapped. These desires entrap us. So the process of temptation begins with us being drawn away by our own desires, then we're entrapped by them.

Next—this is really creepy—desire conceives. The Greek word for "conceived" means we become seized. So the process begins with being dragged away, to being entrapped, to now we're captured. The imagery is intentionally frightening. Did you notice what is now taking place? The process of temptation spirals out of control as we allow our desires to control us, rather than us controlling our desires.

> *The process of temptation spirals out of control as we allow our desires to control us, rather than us controlling our desires*

Afterwards, when the seizing takes place, when that desire conceives, it "gives birth to sin." At this point in the process, sin now comes into play.

Subsequently, sin grows (now this *really* sounds like a horror movie). Eventually sin becomes "full-grown."

Finally, when fully grown, sin "brings forth death." But notice, it all begins with us. It all begins with our own desires.

Not Much Has Changed Over the Millennia

We can take this process all the way back to the very beginning, to the first recorded temptation of man and woman in the Garden of Eden.

God told Adam he could fully enjoy eating of every tree in the garden paradise, except he was not to eat of the tree of the knowledge of good and evil because if he did, he would die. Overall, not a bad deal. And he even got a wife, Eve, out of it too!

Then, of course, the serpent shows up to ruin everything. He and Eve go back and forth, she tells him the rules, to which the serpent replies,

"You will not surely die. For God knows that in the day you eat of it your eyes will be opened, and you will be like God, knowing good and evil" (Genesis 3:4-5).

From there it's a downward slope as verse 6 continues,

"So when the woman saw that the tree was good for food, that it was pleasant to the eyes, and a tree desirable to make one wise, she took of its fruit and ate. She also gave to her husband with her, and he ate."

The Genesis account of the Fall of man mirrors what John wrote in First John 2:16. Look what happens when we overlap these two scriptures,

"For all that is in the world—the lust of the flesh [the tree was good for food], *the lust of the eyes* [it was pleasant to the eyes], *and the pride of life* [a tree desirable to make one wise]*—is not of the Father but is of the world."*

Again, temptation originates in our own desires. Satan's words would have fallen on deaf ears if Eve hadn't thought the fruit was "good...pleasant...and desirable," but she did.

So his lies resonated with her desires and she was tempted.

Now, obviously it could have stopped right there. Eve could have surrendered those desires over to God and shut the whole thing down. But as we know the story goes, she acted on her desires and the end result led to sin, then death for her and Adam, and ultimately, for all of humanity after them.

2. Look for the Exit and Use It

Thankfully, we don't have to be controlled by our sinful desires and temptations. If our desires control us, then we've allowed it, but it doesn't have to be that way. There are numerous opportunities to reverse our choices and take control over our desires. Paul encourages us in First Corinthians 10:13,

"No temptation has overtaken you except such as is common to man; but God is faithful, who will not allow you to be tempted beyond what you are able, but with the temptation will also make the way of escape, that you may be able to bear it."

On the pathway from desire to temptation, there will always be a "way of escape." In fact, there will likely be many opportunities to reverse course.

I compare starting down the wrong path to accidentally getting on the wrong freeway. We've all done it, and when it happens, we're not trapped, right? It's not necessary to alter the destination ("Sorry kids, we're not going to

Disneyland after all!"), just get off at the next exit, turn around, and get back on the right freeway. There are plenty of off ramps to turn around and get back on track. So when we face temptation, quickly get off at the first exit before going any further.

Genesis 39:12 tells us that Joseph "fled" when Potiphar's wife tried to seduce him. Don't stick around to see where the path leads, just get off it! And if we fail by falling for the temptation and sinning, then praise God that all is not lost because we have the opportunity to repent and be forgiven as well.

The important thing to remember is we are not trapped in a cycle of desire to death. We are not involuntarily strapped into a roller coaster of rebellion against God. Quite the opposite, actually. We've been freed from that cycle and we no longer have to fall for the trap.

Small Compromises Lead to Bigger Ones

Another reason to utilize the first "way of escape" available is because small compromises inevitably lead to much bigger ones. Big compromises are much easier to see and therefore avoid. That's the reason why smaller compromises are so dangerous, because they are the ones that are easy to justify and ignore.

An easy example is a married individual who genuinely believes they would never commit adultery. *I would never cheat on my spouse!* But then at work there is an attractive person who gives some positive attention and the good feelings are lingered upon. A small compromise. Then the attractive person wants to have lunch. *Let's have lunch alone, you and me. Let's go grab a bite to eat.* Seems innocent enough. It could even be justified on some level if there is a rush and no one else is around. *I have to eat anyway. Why eat alone?* Another compromise.

Maybe it was someone else's life, or perhaps your own, but we all know where this seemingly innocent path leads. That little lunch leads to spending time together outside of work. That time outside of work leads to a relationship, and before the married individual knows it, they're doing something they sincerely thought they would never do.

How did this happen? If adultery had just presented itself right out the gate, it probably would have been shut down. Cheating as step one would have been unthinkable! Instead, it was those tiny compromises that eventually led to doing things that were previously thought impossible. The shocking thing is the regularity of all kinds of small compromises we often don't see. We must keep a discerning eye on what appear to be innocuous desires and temptations that barely register on our consciousness.

Thankfully, God always gives us a "way of escape," but it's our choice whether we will use it.

3. Don't Roll Over, Put Up a Fight

If we compare Genesis 3:1-6 where Adam and Eve were tempted by Satan, and Matthew 4:1-11 where Jesus was tempted by Satan, we can observe two different approaches with two completely different outcomes. Adam and Eve, according to the text, didn't even resist the temptation. It's like they just rolled over and went along with it. On the other hand, Jesus resisted Satan's lies and He never sinned. As always, He is our perfect example.

Don't submit to your enemy—put up a fight and resist him! James 4:7 exhorts us,

"Therefore submit to God. Resist the devil and he will flee from you."

That's a promise verse right there. If we resist Satan, he *will* flee. Because we're resisting from a position of victory in Christ, Satan has no choice—he *must* flee. That's a promise we can bank on and need to consistently employ.

> *Because we're resisting from a position of victory in Christ, Satan has no choice—he must flee*

So how can we resist a powerful, spiritual being? This brings us to our final two points in overcoming temptation in trials through choosing a position of victory.

4. Speak the Word of God with Authority

I'm pretty sure Jesus wasn't a wimp. The combination of His trade as a carpenter, along with His nomadic, outdoor lifestyle meant that He was physically fit and strong. And that's just addressing His humanity. As the Son of God, He was invincible. Therefore, when we consider how to resist Satan, there is no better model than Jesus. So perhaps the best way to phrase our question is how did Jesus overcome temptation and resist the devil?

Remember, the Gospels never claim to be an exhaustive account of everything Jesus said and did. In fact, John quite candidly and honestly reveals to us,

"And there are also many other things that Jesus did, which if they were written one by one, I suppose that even the world itself could not contain the books that would be written" (John 21:25).

This means that every account in Scripture is there deliberately and intentionally by the will of God. The Bible is the best of the best, most relevant information God wants us to have. And right there in the opening chapters of Matthew, we get a behind the scenes account of Jesus battling Satan face to face.

How did Jesus fight against His (and our) enemy? By speaking the truth of the Word of God, against Satan's lies and deceptions. Our sneak peek into this cosmic battle begins in Matthew 4:1,

"Then Jesus was led up by the Spirit into the wilderness to be tempted by the devil."

Notice who led Him up there. The Spirit led Him up there. For what purpose? For Him to endure that temptation, and to show us how. The Spirit didn't tempt Jesus, but led Him into a situation where temptation was present.

"And when He had fasted forty days and forty nights, afterward He was hungry. Now when the tempter [notice Satan is called the tempter] *came to Him, he said, 'If You are the Son of God, command that these stones become bread'" (verses 2-3).*

On the surface, what was Satan appealing to? He was appealing to Jesus' physical hunger, which wasn't a sinful desire. Jesus was naturally hungry, a legitimate physical need, not a sinful one. So Satan challenged Jesus to turn stones into bread, but what he was really tempting Him to do was to use His deity to work a miracle for His own *personal* benefit.

"But He answered and said, 'It is written, "Man shall not live by bread alone, but by every word that proceeds from the mouth of God."' Then the devil took Him up into the holy city, set Him on the pinnacle of the temple, and said to Him, 'If You are the Son of God, throw Yourself down. For it is written: "He shall give His angels charge over you..."' (verses 4-6).

Isn't it interesting how Satan keeps calling Jesus' deity into question? He says "If You are the Son of God" over and over. Like a prize fighter talking trash, these were subtle jabs intended to get in Jesus' head and throw Him off.

Then Satan changes his strategy. Mimicking Jesus' lead, Satan then begins to quote Scripture, except (of course) he uses it out of context.

"Jesus said to him, 'It is written again, "You shall not tempt the Lord your God."' Again, the devil took Him up on an exceedingly high mountain, and showed Him all the kingdoms of the world and their glory. And he said to Him, 'All these things I will give You if You will fall down and worship me.' Then Jesus said to him 'Away with you, Satan! For it is written, "You shall worship the Lord your God, and Him only you shall serve."' Then the devil left Him, and behold, angels came and ministered to Him" (verses 7-11).

I am convinced this account is in the Bible so that we can learn how to resist Satan, but also to observe the enemy's tactics. Satan tries to deceive us by tempting us when we're physically and emotionally weak, he questions the authority of God, and he twists God's Word out of context.

The Bible isn't a regular book; it's the very breath of God on printed page, and it's a weapon

---

Conversely, Jesus fought Satan by properly using the authority of God's Word. Don't underestimate the power of using Bible verses to overcome temptation and sin. Remember, the Bible isn't a regular book; it's the very breath of God on printed page, and it's a weapon! In Ephesians 6:17, Paul refers to it as,

"The sword of the Spirit, which is the word of God."

After three times getting rebuked with scripture, Satan slunk off and left Him alone. It worked for Jesus, and it will work for us as well.

5. Pray Like You've Never Prayed Before

On the night Jesus was betrayed, He took His disciples to pray with Him in the Garden of Gethsemane. He knew what awaited Him (and them), and He also knew there was only one way to adequately prepare for it. So Jesus instructed them in Luke 22:40,

"Pray that you may not enter into temptation."

When they fell asleep, He woke them and said again in verse 46,

"Why do you sleep? Rise and pray, lest you enter into temptation."

We can pray that God would guard our hearts from temptation. In fact, Jesus modeled such a prayer. You may remember these words from Matthew 6:13, a portion of the Lord's Prayer,

"And do not lead us into temptation, but deliver us from the evil one."

Jesus was instructing His followers to direct that request to the Father. Lead us away from temptation and save us from Satan's snares.

We are not victims to our base desires and the enemy's

deceits. Recognize that temptation begins with our own selfish desires, but we can escape temptation, we can fight, we can employ God's Word as a weapon, and we can pray for strength and deliverance.

From Victory, Not for Victory

As suffering and hardship, trials and tribulations, turn up the heat in the furnace of our lives, temptation will inevitably come flooding in. Temptation to be fearful, hopeless, and angry at God and others. Temptation to circle the wagons around your camp, to isolate, and distrust those around you. Temptation to take matters into your own hands. Temptation to lose faith.

Don't do it. Don't take the bait. You have a warrior Spirit in you. You're not fighting *for* victory; you're fighting *from* victory. Own the position you've been given—a position of victory. The choice is yours. You already have everything you need.

13

Changing Our Position

In the animated movie, *A Bug's Life*, a colony of ants live in fear due to their subjugation by a roving band of grasshoppers. Every year, the ants toil through the summer to gather winter food for the grasshoppers. Through a chain of events, one of the ants, named Flik, inadvertently stands up to the grasshoppers after accidentally losing their harvest. After humiliating Flik, the leader of the grasshoppers, Hopper, gives the ants a second chance to gather them food.

While vacationing the remainder of the summer months away in Mexico, a few of the grasshoppers petition Hopper to remain there for the winter; after all, they have plenty of food and who cares about one little ant taking a stand?

Hopper gets angry and responds, "You let one ant stand up to us, then they all might stand up. Those puny little ants outnumber us a hundred to one. And if they ever figure that out, there goes our way of life!"

That's a cartoon conflict, but the principle is very real, and what's on the line for each party is their way of life.

Satan lost his power over us at the foot of the cross, and he can't ever get it back, unless we voluntarily relinquish our freedom back to him. However, if we do that, we'll be like the ants who technically have the upper hand (and Satan knows it), but choose to live in defeat and surrender. This is not God's will for us.

In John 10:10, Jesus presents two alternative ways of life for us—one from Satan, and the other from Him,

"The thief [Satan] *does not come except to steal, and to kill, and to destroy. I have come that they may have life, and that they may have it more abundantly."*

The abundant life—that's what Jesus offers us. It's a life of freedom from the shackles of sin, forgiveness, and eternal fellowship with God. It's a life out from under the enemy's thumb, and instead in God's loving embrace. This is something God has already given us, but it's up to us to actually live it out.

So what can we practically do to live out our position of victory? What can be done to help us choose the right position to walk in?

1. See Ourselves the Way God Sees Us

I know I'm dating myself, but my very first job after high school was at Blockbuster Video. I was an ambitious 18-year-old and I wanted to look grown up, so I asked my supervisor if I could wear a tie and a button-up shirt. Basically, that was the attire of a supervisor; the regular employees wore polo shirts. He looked at me with a funny expression on his face (I think he was over wearing a tie himself), and granted me permission.

I don't know if I carried myself differently, or if customers were confused, but either way immediately people began treating me differently (an unexpected outcome to me). Whereas in the past, customers would question me if they didn't like an answer I gave them, once I started "dressing up," nobody questioned my judgment anymore. Even my co-workers, who were my peers, treated me better! It was almost as if people viewed me differently based on the way I dressed. Or, like I said, maybe the way I viewed myself changed.

I accidentally learned a powerful lesson through that experience—how we present ourselves to the world changes how people view us, and even how we view ourselves.

This is a theme that resonates with the human soul, which is why it is a common plot in books and movies. From Neo in *The Matrix* discovering that he is "the one," to Rapunzel in Disney's *Tangled* learning she's a lost princess, there is something about the common person discovering they are unbelievably more special or powerful than they originally thought that inspires us.

Why? Hear me in this—I believe this is a universally powerful message because it echoes the biblical story of each one of us. We were all once lost sinners, estranged from our Creator, but as a result of the completed work of Christ, we've been redeemed and called children of God.

We no longer have to walk with our heads down in defeat; instead, we can walk with our heads held high in victory, not based on what we've done, but based on what Jesus has done. When we begin to view ourselves the way He views us, a powerful transformation in our attitude, habits, and lifestyle takes place.

> *We no longer have to walk with our heads down in defeat; instead, we can walk with our heads held high in victory, not based on what we've done, but based on what Jesus has done*

So how does God see us? Who does He say we are? We're told in Romans 8:16-17,

"The Spirit Himself bears witness with our spirit that we are children of God, and if children, then heirs—heirs of God and joint heirs with Christ, if indeed we suffer with Him, that we may also be glorified together."

We are called children of God and heirs of God. We may be poor on this earth, but we are wealthy in the kingdom of heaven! And because He is the King of Kings and the Lord of Lords, that means we are royalty as well. Peter tells us in First Peter 2:9,

"But you are a chosen generation, a royal priesthood, a holy nation, His own special people, that you may proclaim the praises of Him who called you out of darkness into His marvelous light."

I'm sure you've heard the saying, "it's not what you know,

it's who you know." Or the importance of having "friends in high places." You want to talk about knowing the right people? Check out what Jesus said in John 15:14-15,

"You are My friends if you do whatever I command you. No longer do I call you servants, for a servant does not know what his master is doing; but I have called you friends, for all things I heard from My Father I have made known to you."

So not only are we children of God, royalty in His kingdom, but He even calls us His friends. That's who we are in Christ.

The world may say that you're a nobody, but God says you're a somebody. You may feel weak and defeated, but God says you're a super-conqueror! And let me say this, it matters far less what you and others think of yourself, and far more what God thinks of you.

Choosing a position of victory begins with seeing ourselves the way God sees us. The next step is to walk worthy of that calling.

2. Walk Worthy of the Calling

I guarantee that if you suddenly discovered you had inherited millions of dollars, or that you were royalty, there would certainly be some significant changes in your life! Why? Because you will inevitably view yourself differently in light of that new information.

The same thing is true for us as children of God. Now that

we know who we are in Christ, we should start acting differently. We need to live up to the new status that God has granted us.

It is in speaking to this transformation that Paul exhorts the Church, in Ephesians 4:1,

"I, therefore, the prisoner of the Lord, beseech you to walk worthy of the calling with which you were called."

Walk worthy of the calling! In other words, our actions need to be consistent with our identity. What would you think of a soldier who doesn't know how to fire a gun, a chef who doesn't know their way around a kitchen, or a computer programmer who doesn't know how to turn on a computer? These inconsistencies would lead you to conclude there was definitely something wrong.

Part of our calling, as it relates to a position of victory, is to walk ready for the spiritual battle that is presented to us daily. We need to put on our uniform and confidently head into battle, knowing we're already on the winning side and have been fully equipped for the challenge ahead.

Ephesians 6:10-11 reminds us,

"Finally, my brethren, be strong in the Lord and in the power of His might. Put on the whole armor of God, that you may be able to stand against the wiles of the devil."

Notice, our strength and power are not our own, they are both from the Lord. The armor to stand against Satan and his attacks has already been given to us. We currently possess everything we need to be successful, but it's our choice whether or not to use the resources God has given us.

I've often imagined what it might be like to win a shopping spree at Home Depot and be able to basically mirror their entire tool section in my garage. Every type of power tool imaginable, right there, ready to be used for any project that may present itself! But what if I never opened any of the packages and just left the tools in their boxes? What difference would it make to have them if I didn't use them? It would almost be like not having them at all.

I'm happy to announce that you and I have already won the ultimate shopping spree! Philippians 4:19 reminds us,

"And my God shall supply all your need according to His riches in glory by Christ Jesus."

We have every tool we need...we just need to use them.

So no matter what life throws your way, choose a position of victory. You've been given a new identity in Christ, you've been fully equipped for the battle, and the best news is the battle has already been won by Him!

"These things I have spoken to you, that in Me you may have peace. In the world you will have tribulation; but be of good cheer, I have overcome the world."

– John 16:33

Epilogue

As I stated at the beginning of this book, the COVID-19 pandemic has been a world-changing event, which has certainly affected all our lives in some way, but it certainly won't be the last. We're given the reason in First John 2:17 as a sobering reminder,

"The world is passing away, and the lust of it; but he who does the will of God abides forever."

This world, as we know it, is moving toward a final conclusion where the Lord will return and once and for all claim what is rightfully His. Until then, the world fades, but we abide.

Don't ever forget that we are victorious warriors, children of the King, and we have no reason to mirror the world's hopelessness and fear during seasons of great difficulty. Yes, we suffer and hurt no different, but our attitude and outlook should absolutely be different. When those who don't know Jesus look at us, they should see the hope we have in Him.

In Revelation 22:12-13, Jesus says,

"Behold, I am coming quickly, and My reward is with Me, to give to every one according to his work. I am the Alpha and the Omega, the Beginning and the End, the First and the Last."

The sand in the hourglass is running out. We're in the

fourth quarter and the two-minute warning has rung. This can be, should be, and I believe *will* be the Church's finest hour. If only we will choose a healthy attitude and biblical perspective during times of adversity.

So let's choose a heart of thankfulness, a mindset of joy, and a position of victory.

Finally, I love Paul's admonition in Romans 13:11-12. May it ring true in our hearts and resonate in our souls,

"And do this, knowing the time, that now it is high time to awake out of sleep; for now our salvation is nearer than when we first believed. The night is far spent, the day is at hand. Therefore let us cast off the works of darkness, and let us put on the armor of light."

The choice is ours. Choose wisely...

Acknowledgments

I'd like to thank my wife, Juanita, and our children, Skylar and Maksim. Through life's trials and tribulations, your company helps me remain thankful, joyful, and victorious.

Andrew Enos, my friend, brother, and kindred spirit; thank you for your faithfulness and wisdom all these years. It's a privilege to share life and ministry with you, and I pray we get to do so for many more years to come.

McKenna Hafner, thank you for your commitment to Abundant Harvest Publishing, and making every project, especially mine, better than they otherwise would be. You truly are an editor extraordinaire!

Hector and Florence Placencia, your gift of transcription is much appreciated. Your humility and obedience to serve simply as an act of worship is inspiring.

And as always, thank You, Lord, for allowing me the opportunity and gift of writing. You placed this message heavy on my heart. I pray my humble attempt to do it justice honors You and blesses others.

About the Author

Erik V. Sahakian has committed his life to serving Jesus Christ through teaching God's inerrant Word, ministering to the body of Christ, and writing. He joyfully worships and serves with his wife and children at Wildwood Calvary Chapel in Yucaipa, CA.

Visit www.eriksahakian.com to learn more.